Machine Quilting In Sections

Don't Finish Another Quilt Until You Read This Book!

Marti Michell

From Marti Michell
P.O. Box 80218
Atlanta, GA 30366-0218
www.frommarti.com

About the Author

In 1972, Marti Michell's patchwork hobby suddenly emerged as a patchwork kit business. For nearly 14 years, Yours Truly, Inc., a premiere company in quiltmaking and fabric crafts, was owned by Marti and her husband, Richard. In 1985, the company was sold and Marti began writing books and designing fabrics, patterns and tools for several major companies in the quilting industry.

At the 1991 International Quilt Market in Houston, Marti's efforts and successes were recognized by her peers. She was selected to receive the first Michael Kile Award of Achievement, "honoring commitment to creativity and excellence in the quilting industry."

Marti is internationally recognized as an author, teacher and innovator of strip techniques and rotary cutting methods. She can cut nearly any straight-sided geometric shape with a good acrylic ruler and a rotary cutter. That did not prevent her from falling in love with the concept of actual-size acrylic templates for rotary cutting. From MARTI MICHELL Perfect Patchwork Templates were introduced in 1995.

Marti has embraced the concept of machine quilting in sections since the mid-1970s. In this book, she has collected her favorite techniques to share with you.

The Michells have two grown children. Jeff, a computer engineer, lives with his family in Seattle, WA, and Stacy, a quilting industry entrepreneur, owns Shades Hand-dyed Textiles and lives in Atlanta, GA. Richard and Marti are currently being greeted by one guard cat when they arrive home in suburban Atlanta, GA.

In 2004, Marti was honored to be designated as the Silver Star honoree by Quilts, Inc. Most recently, Marti was selected as the 2020 inductee into the Quilters Hall of Fame.

Acknowledgments

It takes many people to complete a project of this size. For this book, my gratitude goes to all of the people who contributed to the invention of the sewing machine, as well as those who have developed it into the wonderful tool it is today.

It is especially important to acknowledge and thank those who have been directly involved in the creation of this book. There are several guest projects featured and those designers are duly recognized in the text. The rest of the projects were designed and made in my studio.

Quilting Projects
For design assistance, special thanks to Ann Davis Mahaffey. The quilting and sewing assistance of these Marti Michell Studio associates was greatly appreciated: Ann Cookston, Martha Dudley, Harriett Fox, Joyce Gary, Sheri Gravel, Jennifer Kay, Pam Lillethun, Camellia Pesto, and Ellen Rosintoski.

Book Production
The editorial assistance of Kathy O'Meara Magnuson, Joyce Gary, Patti Bachelder and Jenny Lynn Price made completing the text a more pleasant task. Words become a complete instructional book with good illustration and photography. Patti Bachelder and Ann Davis Mahaffey have once again contributed accurate and attractive illustrations. Stacy Michell had both a good eye and good ideas as she assisted in photo styling.

Photography was done by Steve Rucker of Bread and Butter Studio, Atlanta, GA.

Book design was done by Patti Bachelder.

Published by From MARTI MICHELL
Michell Marketing, Inc.
P. O. Box 80218, Atlanta, GA 30366

Printed in the U.S.A.

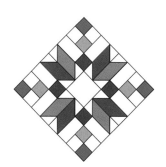

Table of Contents

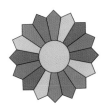

Low-Carb Quilting

It's all About Reducing Bulk for Machine Quilters

Low-carb is all the rage; why not low-carb quilting? The goal of this book is to help make machine quilting more manageable by showing effective, creative and successful ways to:

- machine quilt in sections;

- assemble the sections successfully;

- and/or reduce the bulk of the quilt in some other way.

This book has been written to encourage people who are machine quilting to consider alternative methods of assembling their quilts. It is a book about machine quilting in sections and assembling the sections.

If you are making a quilt right now, please do not add any borders without reading Chapter 1.

Typically, borders are added to a quilt before layering and quilting, which means folding or rolling the quilt to make it small enough to feed under the sewing machine needle for quilting. The good news is, the easiest way to reduce the size of your quilt for machine quilting is to quilt the center section before adding the borders. The difference in the volume between a quilt with borders and without borders is immense. This book offers options for quilting the interior section of a quilt and then adding and quilting the borders, as well as a method for adding already quilted borders.

In fact, some of the methods in this book may be appealing to hand quilters because they reduce the size and weight of the section being quilted.

The quilting referred to in this book is the epitome of "quilt as desired." That means there is no discussion about quilting designs or how to mark them, et cetera. Chapter 6 includes basic layering and quilting instructions, but in reality, this is not a "how to machine quilt" book. It is about dividing the quilt into sections and, in some cases, the implications that might have for your quilting designs. There are full instructions for several quilts, however, instructions are not given for all quilts shown. If there are no instructions, a source is given whenever possible, so you can locate specific instructions for a quilt that is shown. However, it is our intention that you will apply the information to quilts you are making or want to make.

One of the most frequently asked questions about machine quilting is, "Do I need a fancy machine?" Need is an interesting word. Does your spouse need a riding lawn mower or a fishing boat? My best answer is that if you are pleased with the piecing you do on your current machine, it will probably be just fine for machine quilting. However, you do need a machine that can easily do free-motion quilting and has a good "walking foot," either built-in or as an accessory.

Perhaps the only thing you think you want to know about machine quilting is "How do you get a great big quilt through that little hole?" We will repeatedly say "Divide your quilt into smaller sections and it will go through the hole much more easily." You may as well accept the fact that no household sewing machine has an opening as large as you want!

My Personal Progression to Machine Quilting in Sections

When I was a garment sewer, I loved both the machine work and the hand work involved. When I started quilting in 1969, the prevailing attitude was that a quilt wasn't a real quilt unless it was hand-quilted. I didn't question it; I loved handwork so I did hand quilting. In 1972, my husband and I started Yours Truly, Inc., a company that produced patchwork kits and other products for quilters. My life changed dramatically and time for hand quilting was a thing of the past. For a few years I denied that reality, then I began developing Quilt-As-You-Sew methods. While this was a compromise of sorts, it was a good compromise for me because it combined the actual process of quilting with the machine piecing I enjoyed so much. I went to great lengths to make sure none of the tell-tale machine quilting showed on the top of my quilts so they would be real quilts.

In March of 1977, a Log Cabin quilt I made using this method was featured in *Woman's Day* magazine. *Woman's Day* offered the quilt in kit form and heralded it as "The Quickest Quilt in the World." It is not unusual for quiltmakers to tell me that it was the first quilt they made. It was extremely popular. In fact, it was repeated in five color combinations during the next five years. It even made the cover once, as you can see in the photo below.

Since that *Woman's Day* magazine offer, I have developed many Quilt-As-You-Sew techniques. (To better describe both the technique and the result, I have even changed the name from Quilt-As-You-Sew to Quilt-As-You-Piece.) In 1991, ASN Publishing asked me to rewrite the Log Cabin technique and called the book *Weekend Log Cabin Quilts*.

In the intervening years, attitudes about machine quilting had changed dramatically. Free-motion machine quilting had come of age in the mid-1980s and at the end of that decade, machine-quilted quilts were winning coveted Best of Show prizes. As a result, I made some changes to update the original instructions.

Instead of every seam being a stitch and flip technique, I chain-pieced the center square and first four strips before centering them on the batting and backing. Since it was now an option to have visible machine quilting, I could secure the center square with some quick free-motion quilting. Instead of trying to tuck under raw edges of joined blocks, a step universally dreaded by everyone who tried it, I began to cover raw seams with finishing strips, described in this book on page 22.

As visible machine quilting became acceptable among quilters, it was obvious that the same techniques I had used for assembling Quilt-As-You-Sew quilted blocks could be used successfully with larger sections of a quilt. Most people who machine quilt have no difficulty

quilting a wall hanging or crib quilt. So why not think about quilting big quilts in small sections?

Every quilter knows that typically a quilt will have raw edges and typically those edges are bound. So, if you divide a quilt top and quilt it in smaller sections, whether the sections are blocks, quarters of the quilt or strips, there will be more raw edges. I have quilted in sections since 1976 and have included techniques in many patterns and books. However, sometime in the late 1990s I noticed a demand for consolidated information. If one of my classes or lectures included any quilt that was machine quilted in sections, that was the topic that people wanted me to explain. This book is the response to those requests.

Machine Quilting in Sections and You

My hope is that machine quilting in sections will be the machine quilting solution you've been seeking. Read through the entire book, even skimming the quilt patterns, to become familiar with the options for different styles of quilts. One word of caution—for most people these are new techniques. Just like anything else, you may not be as happy with your first try as your second or third. With just a little practice, you will find it a natural and easy way to successfully finish your quilts.

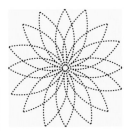

Why People Want to Machine Quilt in Sections

Machine quilting has come into its own. People are doing it because they want to, not as a substitute for hand quilting. Gradually, people are understanding that machine quilting is a different skill than hand quilting. It is not easier than hand quilting, it is only faster.

So why is machine quilting enjoying such popularity?

Because it is fast. The most common reason people turn to machine quilting is speed. As quiltmakers produce quilt tops abundantly, the commonsense approach of quilting by machine enters the picture.

Because it is very durable. In addition to being practical, the durability of machine quilting makes a lot of sense when it comes to quilting a crib quilt, a college dorm quilt or any quilt that needs repeated washing.

Because it is more realistic for most gift giving. Most people find it is difficult to really give a quilt away if they have spent weeks hand quilting it. If you have ever given away a hand-quilted quilt, but you still think of it as "my quilt," you are one of those people. If you think someone may not appreciate the number of hours you have spent quilting a quilt, you are probably right. These are perfect examples of reasons to machine quilt a gift.

Because free-motion quilting enhances efforts. In the early 1980s, quilters discovered a way to be more creative. They dropped the feed dogs on their sewing machines, and suddenly free-motion traditional decorative designs, like feather quilting, were added to the machine quilting repertoire. At that time, many people still considered it a substitute for hand quilting, but a very beautiful one. It was great fun to listen to people argue at quilt shows about whether certain quilts were or weren't machine-quilted! Especially when you knew they were!

Because fabulous threads add another dimension. The fabulous threads that are available today have added a new dimension to machine quilting. The introduction of invisible thread helped start the run for machine quilting. That was followed by wonderful decorative threads that are meant to be highly visible. Some machine quilting is so elaborate that, to me, it crosses the fine line between machine quilting and machine embroidery.

Because some creative effects are only possible with a machine. One of the most important factors in this quilting evolution (or is it a revolution?) is that quilters have discovered some of the unique qualities and special effects that only machine quilting can provide. More and more people have learned to look at the sewing machine as more than a tool of convenience, but also as a tool of creativity.

Because it is fun to use a sewing machine. There are a lot of people who really love to use their sewing machines, so finding machine quilting, a new thing to do with their machines, has been a perfect match!

Because there are changing attitudes about machine quilting. As machine quilting became both more prevalent and more attractive, attitudes about the acceptance of machine quilting changed. While most quilt shows would not accept a machine-quilted quilt in the 1970s, by the late 1980s several machine-quilted quilts had won Best of Show and Viewer's Choice awards in prestigious shows. This caused a very important shift in attitude. If judges could award top prizes, including top monetary awards, to machine-quilted quilts, then non-competitive quiltmakers could also take pride in their machine-quilted quilts.

Because machine-quilted quilts can be so beautiful!

We just listed some reasons why people want to machine quilt. Now, it is time to add another stipulation:

Why would people want to machine quilt in sections?

Because thinking outside the block is new. If you tried quilting by the block in the 1980s, you know the part you didn't like was putting the blocks together. That is why we have new sizes and new finishing techniques!

Because it is easier. It is easier physically. Quilting in sections means there is some need for another step, the process of finishing seams. This is not a difficult step, but it does take time. This method is not faster than machine quilting the entire quilt; it actually adds a finishing step. However, I don't think it is slower, either, because the quilting process itself is easier and quicker, thereby saving time that can then be used to assemble the quilt sections.

Because it is necessary. Many of us just don't have the arm, shoulder and back strength we once had. Some people will never physically be able to machine quilt anything much larger than a crib quilt. They simply need to plan ahead. With almost every quilt, there is a way to quilt in sections no larger than a crib quilt.

Because it opens new avenues. Quilting in sections often allows the quilter to use a quilting technique, such as elaborate feather quilting, they simply couldn't use otherwise on a full-size quilt.

Because it is fun to use different backing fabrics on each section. More and more, I use pieced backings for my quilts. Because I am machine quilting, I don't need to worry about seams in the backing adding bulk in the way a hand quilter might. I like pieced backs because I don't have to buy six or seven yards of one fabric. When quilting in sections, I can use a different fabric on each section, or for a very scrappy look I can piece the backing for each section.

Because it is fun to finish your quilts. Who knows how many bed-size quilt tops remain unquilted because many quilters cannot imagine machine quilting an entire quilt? Quilting in sections may be the way you ease into quilting an entire bed-size quilt, or you may decide quilting in sections is perfect for all your quilts.

Because it takes less space. To efficiently machine quilt a full-size bed quilt, it is almost mandatory to have extra tables around the sewing machine table to support the bulk of the quilt as you work. The luxury of extra tables and the space for them is not required when quilting in sections.

Because it is less expensive than sending quilt tops out to be quilted—and that may be the bottom line.

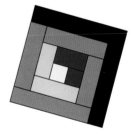

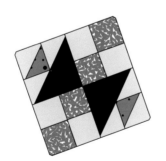

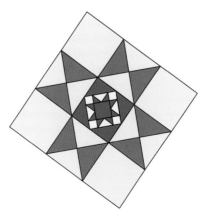

Chapter 1

Border Control

Most borders account for at least 25%–35% of the surface of a quilt. Often, just quilting the interior of the quilt before adding the borders is all that is required to make your quilt manageable for quilting on your own machine. Since borders are always added after the interior of the quilt is completed, it isn't an unusual idea to think of them as separate sections.

A quick way to determine if your quilt is a candidate for border control is to subtract the width of the borders from the finished size of the quilt. That is the size of the interior of the quilt. Often this size, while bigger than a crib quilt, is manageable enough to forget about more divisions.

It is possible that you have the interior section of a quilt top just laying around waiting for you to decide on the borders. If so, you have what you need to start practicing the techniques in this chapter. One of these three techniques will be adaptable to almost any quilt with a border.

Maintain Border Integrity

All of the border control methods detailed in this book are designed to maintain the complete integrity of the borders. No one wants to see a seam cutting across the surface of the quilt border, telegraphing to the world that the quilt was quilted in sections and the pieces were joined after quilting.

Before Cutting Borders

Measurements are generally included for the border widths as shown on a quilt in a given pattern. Think of those measurements as guidelines. Feel free to design or redesign your own borders to make the quilt the size you want and as attractive as possible.

Regardless of the method you choose, it is very important to make sure that your quilt is the same dimension on opposite sides before cutting borders. Measure both the length and width of the quilt in several places, as shown.

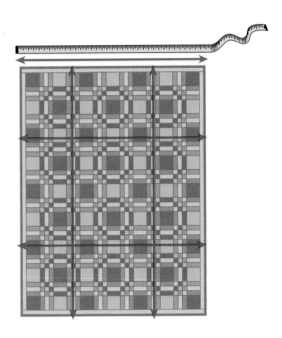

Carefully measure border sections to match the size of the quilt interior. For a smooth finish, the length of the sections to be joined and the dimensions of the quilt must match.

Equalizing Border Lengths

Whenever possible, cut border strips on the lengthwise grain. Cutting this way provides a firmer, less stretchy finish. If you are making blunt corners, cutting side border strips before cutting top and bottom border strips will help equalize the lengths needed and, in many cases, require less yardage.

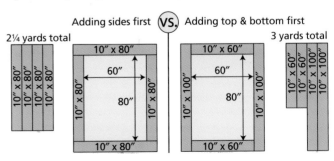

Adding Borders as Sections

Adding Borders by Encasing Raw Edges

Encasing the raw edges with a six-layer seam (three layers each, quilt and border) is the simplest way to add borders to a quilted interior section. This is the method I developed in 1976 for the Quilt-As-You-Sew Log Cabin quilt in *Woman's Day* magazine (see page 5) when polyester batting was the batting of choice. It is generally light and fluffy and when polyester batting is sewn into a seam it can be trimmed and pressed into submission. If you are using cotton batting, read page 10 before continuing.

A six-layer-seam border encloses the raw edges of the quilted interior as part of the process of adding the first border to the quilt. If there are more borders, they are added using a stitch and flip technique (see below). If there is to be additional quilting on the borders, it is usually done after all the borders are added. Even though the quilt is then full size, the borders are the only area being quilted; the rest of the quilt is to the left of the needle. The method results in blunt corners, not mitered, so plan accordingly.

Preparing the Borders, Border Batting and Border Backing

Border lengths are determined by the size of the unquilted quilt top and subsequent borders. Widths are personal choices that affect the length of the remaining borders. The border batting and border backing strips must be as wide as the total finished width of all the finished quilt border widths plus a 1½" allowance for machine quilting.

Adding the First Border

1. Lay the quilted interior on a large flat surface, right side up. Put one of the first side borders on top of the quilt, right side down and long edges aligned. Mark and match the center and quarter points of both the quilt and the border. Pin in place sparingly.

2. To add the batting and border backing fabric, fold the edge of the quilt forward about 15". Lay the border

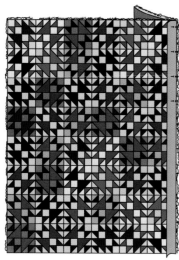

backing fabric against the backing of the quilt, right sides together. Put the batting on top of it. Align the raw edges and the ends. Pin securely in place through all layers.

3. Machine stitch ¼" from the raw edges, through all six layers, the entire length of the quilt. Remove all pins.

4. Repeat steps one, two and three on the opposite side of the quilt.

5. Trim away any excess batting from the seams to reduce bulk, but do not trim closer than ⅛" or the batting will tend to pull out of the seam. Pull the front border, batting, and border backing away from the quilt interior and bring them together so they are flat on the same surface. The batting is now sandwiched between the border and the border backing fabric. This is one seam I recommend pressing, preferably with steam.

6. Position the crosswise pieces of the first border, border backing, and batting. The batting and border backing strips go the full width of the quilt. The border fabrics stop even with the outer edges of the side border strips. Trim the ends of the border strips to exact length.

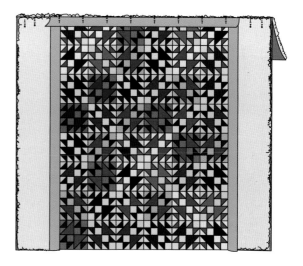

7. Pin the first strip securely. Machine stitch and trim the excess batting from the seam allowance. Pull the border, batting and border backing away from the quilt interior, as before. Press the seam flat. Repeat on the other end to finish the first border.

Adding Subsequent Borders with the Stitch and Flip Method

Adding subsequent borders is quick and easy with the stitch and flip method. Attach the side strips before the top and bottom strips. Finish adding one border before starting the next.

1. Pin the first border flat. Along one long edge, place a strip of the second border fabric on top of the first border, right sides facing and raw edges matching, and pin them securely. The ends of the second border's side strips should line up with the sides of the first end border.

2. Machine stitch through both layers of fabric, the batting and the backing fabric, ¼″ from the raw edges of the two border pieces. Align and stitch the second border strip to the opposite side of the quilt in the same manner. After removing the pins, pull the second border forward to lie flat on the batting. Press.

3. Add border strips to the top and bottom of the quilt to complete the second border. These strips go from one end of the second side border to the other.

4. Repeat for remaining borders.

Cotton Batting and the Six-Layer Seam

Cotton batting, compared to polyester, is very dense. When two layers of cotton batting are sewn into a seam, it is quite stiff and bulky. As I began to use cotton batting more often, I rarely used the six-layer seam method. Then one day I had a Eureka! moment. For years I thought I had to include the batting in the seam to prevent it from balling up at the edge of the border when the quilt was washed. Suddenly, I realized I could eliminate the layer of border batting from the seam—I would cut the border backing about ⅜″ wider than the batting and sew the batting in place on the backing before those pieces were joined to the quilt interior. Recently I realized I could fuse the batting in place with Marti's Choice Fusible Tape. Follow these steps:

1. Determine the total width and length of the batting pieces. Cut one long side of the batting straight with a ruler and rotary cutter. Fortunately, cotton batting does not squish out of shape like polyester batting.

2. Place the batting on the wrong side of the backing. The straight cut edge should be almost ⅜″ in from the cut edge of the backing fabric. Pin, if desired.

3. Sew the batting to the backing, or fuse it in place with Marti's Choice 1″ Fusible Tape. If you sew, the seam should be ⅜″ from the edge of the backing. The stitching will show on the back of the quilt. The bobbin thread should match the backing fabric. When you choose to fuse, the seam is still technically a six-layer seam, but the Fusible Tape is so thin, it barely counts.

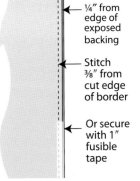

Now this is a five-layer seam—four layers of fabric and one of batting in the seam allowance that encases the raw edges of the quilt interior —but it is a big reduction in bulk.

Reducing to a Four-Layer Seam

Reducing this to just four layers of fabric will be different with almost every quilt top; plan ahead. The key is to quilt enough to secure the quilt top without quilting within the last inch or two of the edge. Then:

1. Trim the batting and backing all around the quilt top, leaving 1″ exposed.

2. Set up a seam guide on your machine so that you can stitch 1⅜″ from the newly-cut edge.

3. Lift the edge of the quilt top to stitch through only the batting and backing, 1⅜″ from the cut edge. This seam will stay in the quilt, so the bobbin thread should match the backing. Stitch around the entire quilt interior.

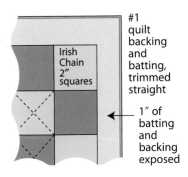

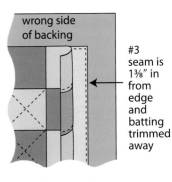

4. Take the quilt interior to the cutting table and fold the backing under the quilt, lift the top out of the way and carefully trim away the batting close to the seam.

OR trim away the excess batting first and use 1″ Marti's Choice Fusible Tape (half on the batting/half on the backing) to fuse batting in place. There will be no stitching so there will not be a line of stitching that shows on the backing.

5. Smooth everything back in place and continue quilting as desired. Trim the backing to size when the quilting is complete—Until then, it is nice to have extra fabric to hold as you quilt. You are now ready to add the first border (page 9).

Now when the sections are joined, step 3 on page 9 would say, "Machine stitch ¼″ from the raw edges, through all *four* layers, the entire length of the quilt."

The Four-Layer Seam or Stitch and Flip

This method is adaptable to nearly any traditionally pieced and layered quilt. The quilt interior is centered on backing and batting that are cut full size. It reduces bulk and weight when machine quilting the interior section of a quilt, and results in a nice finish at the same time.

Traditionally, borders are added to the quilt interior and then the complete quilt top is layered and prepared for quilting. When borders are added using the four-layer seam, only the patchwork interior of the quilt is centered on the full-size backing and batting (cut large enough to eventually allow the total width of all the borders to be added).

After the interior section is quilted, borders are added to the quilt. They are added just as they would have been added to the quilt top traditionally, except that you will sew through the existing batting and backing at the same time. It is the same stitch and flip method used for adding subsequent borders in the six-layer border method. The point is, the one seam used to attach the border fabric to the quilt top performs double duty—it adds the border and does the quilting at the same time. There are additional benefits to using this method:

- It reduces the weight and bulk of the quilt while you are quilting the interior section. You might be surprised how heavy the border fabrics and pins are, or how heavy they seem, when quilting the entire quilt.

- It eliminates trimming and is less bulky. The seam that holds the quilt and borders together in the original Quilt-As-You-Sew or six-layer seam method is thicker and has an extra layer of batting that may require trimming.

- In the six-layer seam method, separate border batting and border backing pieces are measured and cut. With the four-layer seam method, those steps are omitted.

Preparing and Quilting the Quilt Interior

1. Cut the batting and backing 2″ to 4″ bigger all around than the finished size of the quilt. That means the interior plus the finished sizes of all the borders.

2. Do not add the borders to the quilt interior.

3. Lay the backing wrong side up on a large flat surface. Layer the batting on top of the backing. Center the quilt interior right side up on top of the batting and backing, and baste.

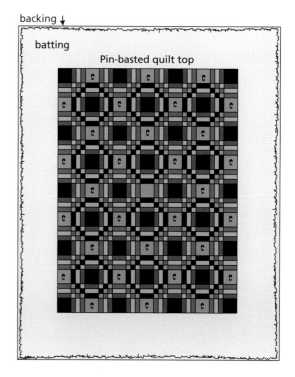

backing ↓
batting
Pin-basted quilt top

4. Roll up the backing and batting and pin to reduce the size of the package you are quilting and to cover the batting. Uncovered batting can be a nuisance catching on pins, watches, et cetera.

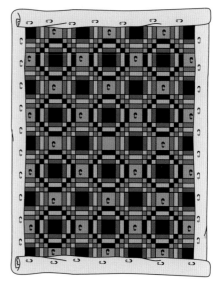

5. Quilt interior as desired.

Adding the Borders

After the quilt interior is quilted, place it right side up on a large flat surface. Remove all of the pins to release the rolled-up batting and backing.

Add the side borders first and then the top and bottom pieces, just as if you were adding borders before layering and quilting, except you will sew through all four layers using the stitch and flip method. When there are several borders, I prefer to add them one fabric at a time to create more quilting in the border sections.

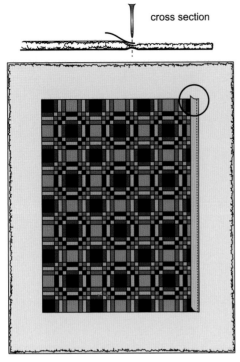

Quilt and seam at the same time.

1. Put the first side border strip right side down on top of the quilt, as shown. Pin in place. Stitch through all thicknesses, quilting and seaming at the same time.

2. Repeat on the opposite side. Open both side strips flat into the finished position. Pin or lightly press the first border flat before seaming across it with another border.

3. Add the top and bottom borders in the same fashion.

Repeat steps 1–3 for all borders. The blunt corners will look better if, on subsequent borders, you continue to add side borders first, then the top and bottom borders.

Attaching Completely Quilted Borders Using Five-, Six- or Eight-Layer Seams

Each border design will need to be treated differently. Perhaps the easiest way to understand this method would be to imagine a lovely cable quilted on a border that will be added separately. Or look at examples, like the Stippled Postage Stamp Basket quilt on page 29. The four corners of the Feathered Heart Wallhanging on page 34 can be thought of as completely quilted borders. Also look at Some Enchanted Evening on page 41. The borders are pieced and part of the five different sections.

If you want to quilt the borders before attaching them, they can be added to the quilt using any appropriate method detailed in Chapter 3. They are simply another individual section of the quilt. Border assembly will be treated just like any other section. See Chapters 3 and 4, especially the Stippled Postage Stamp Basket quilt in Chapter 4.

Measure your quilt to determine the length to cut the borders, backing, and batting strips. Cut the first pair of lengthwise strips (for the sides of the quilt) the exact length of the quilt interior. The length of the top and bottom strips is the width of the quilt top, plus twice the desired finished border width plus ½″ for seam allowances.

Chapter 2

Low-Fat Quilting

In the early 1990s, I knew that machine quilter supreme, Debra Wagner, suggested what I considered an unusual way to reduce bulk when machine quilting. First you would layer the full quilt and full backing with *only the center section of batting*; hence, what I call low-fat quilting. (As you may recall, low-fat dieting was the rage in the '90s.) Next, you would machine quilt the center section and then, using a hand herringbone stitch, piece one side of the batting into its original position, quilt that section and repeat on the final section.

Well, I simply turned a deaf ear to that suggestion. Piecing batting with the hand herringbone stitch was something I had avoided ever since the first time I did it in 1974! Besides, I was satisfied with reducing bulk by machine quilting in sections. However, I occasionally heard people talk about what I call the low-fat method, and as I approached this book, I realized I needed to try it myself and I did. Guess what? I still don't like piecing batting.

However, I don't need to and neither do you! As I quilted and got closer to the dreaded hand-piecing step, I wondered if I could use narrow strips of a very lightweight fusible interfacing to hold my batting pieces together. It worked really well, so for years I recommended buying lightweight non-woven interfacing and cutting it into strips for this technique. It was only in 2011 that we cut it in strips for you and introduced Marti's Choice Fusible Tape available in two widths, 1″ and 2″. When you eliminate the hand stitching, low-fat quilting is a great way to reduce bulk in machine quilting. (As of this printing, Marti's Choice Fusible Tape has been used successfully on cotton, polyester and wool batting.) As with everything, there are advantages and disadvantages.

Disadvantages

- If you don't have Marti's Choice Fusible Tape or some other good lightweight fusible interfacing to hold the cut edges together, you will have to stitch the batting together by hand.

- It can be a little awkward to get the quilt in progress in a good position on the ironing board or other surface for the fusing. One solution combines a large table and an 18″ x 24″ cutting mat that reverses to a padded ironing surface. With the quilt and partial batting sections flat on the table, move the mat, padded side up, along under the area being fused. Put the fusible side of the Fusible Tape down on the batting. Cover with a single layer of cotton fabric, like a press cloth, and steam press in place.

- You need to be sure that you are securely quilting the batting "seam line(s)," just in case the interfacing or long hand stitches come loose when washing.

- The quilting is stop-and-start in many of the seams and other quilting areas because you have to stop quilting until you can reposition the batting.

- The quilt is not as fat or heavy when quilting, but it is still a big quilt top.

Advantages

- The method can be used with nearly any style of quilt.

- You do not have to think or plan ahead. Your quilt top can be complete when you decide to use this method.

- When you are done, there are no surprise seams, no finishing strips or any other telltale evidence that you did not quilt all in one piece.

Reducing Bulk the Low-Fat Way

The technique is really quite simple. Layer the quilt backing, batting and quilt top. Complete the pin basting or other chosen technique down the center third of the quilt.

Pull the top and bottom away and cut batting with a curvy line, at least two inches away from the pinned section. Remove the unpinned section of batting on the right side of the quilt's center. Mark the batting piece with identification so it will easily reassemble with the center section. Repeat on the left side.

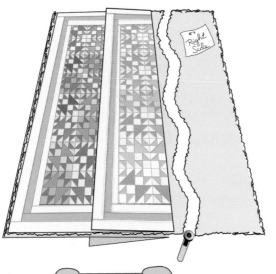

Quilt the first section.

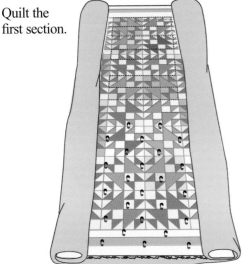

Add back one side of the batting. (If you stitch, I recommend the herringbone stitch, page 18).

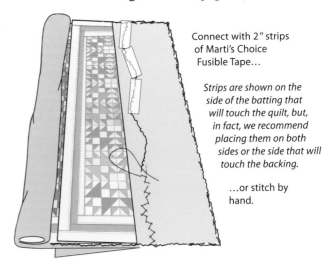

Connect with 2" strips of Marti's Choice Fusible Tape…

Strips are shown on the side of the batting that will touch the quilt, but, in fact, we recommend placing them on both sides or the side that will touch the backing.

…or stitch by hand.

Baste and quilt this section.

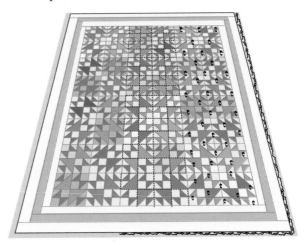

Replace the batting on the other side, then baste and finish quilting.

Low-fat quilting was illustrated with A World Without End. The quilt shown on page 46 was actually quilted in sections as described on pages 47 and 48. However, many quilters will have a completed quilt top and low fat quilting would be a perfect technique for finishing the quilt.

Ask for Marti's Choice Fusible Tape, Product #8221, 2" wide by 30 yards long (1 roll). Also available in these 1" width by 30-yard selections: Product #8272 (1 roll) and Product #8220 (2 rolls).

Quilting the Rose Garden
Hidden Stars Sampler

As I said earlier, I felt the need to try this method and, conveniently, I had a full-size queen/double sampler quilt top, the Rose Garden Hidden Stars, that needed quilting in a hurry. Because I really don't like to piece batting and was resisting the idea, I had decided that, instead of removing batting on both sides of the quilt, I would remove only one-third of the batting on one side of my quilt. I would roll up the non-batting side to quilt the center section. Then I would quilt the side with batting and, finally, I would sew the last section in place and finish the quilting.

As I layered everything in preparation to cut away batting on one side only, it dawned on me that I had a diagonal set quilt and the way Debra had described her method was really only appropriate for a straight set quilt.

Back I went to the planning stage. Whatever amount of batting I was going to remove would need to be cut away diagonally. I still wanted to try removing batting from only one side of the center. The diagram below left shows how much batting I cut away. If I had cut just a little more, the longest diagonal seam would have been less bulky and easier to work with. However, I planned to stitch in the ditch along both sides of the sashing with machine-guided stitching, and I wanted to minimize stop and go points in those seams when possible.

The photo below shows the finished quilt. Once I thought of using very lightweight fusible interfacing to join the sections, I was surprised by how much I liked this method. Even though it was still an 84″ by 105″ quilt, it would roll much more easily. It was, however, still 84″ by 105″ which means that extra table support around my sewing machine was very helpful, almost mandatory.

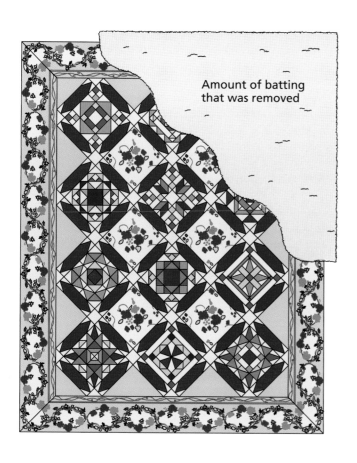

Amount of batting that was removed

Finished Rose Garden Hidden Stars

Chapter 3

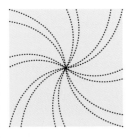

Quilting Big Quilts in Small Sections

Planning the Division

In this chapter, we begin to look at solutions above and beyond Border Control or Low-Fat Quilting. Any quilt that has straight seams somewhere is a candidate for quilting in sections. However, it is very important that quilting by the section be planned before you even start piecing. Once a quilt top is completely put together, most people are unwilling to remove seams to divide the top so it can be quilted in sections! If you are following instructions in a book or pattern, you will almost always need to read ahead and make notations of simple changes in the instructions. For example, mark the sections you don't want to join.

Every quilt is different.

There is not one solution that works for every quilt. Instead, quilting in sections requires individual planning. At the same time, there are so many similarities in quilt layouts that soon you will be able to look at a picture and quickly identify likely divisions. After you have read further in this book, spend a little time looking through any quilt magazine or book and practice identifying ways to divide a quilt.

The earliest machine quilting in sections was divided into single blocks. This method involves many seams that require finishing. Every step that can be eliminated will save time. The logical conclusion is to quilt larger sections and have fewer seams to finish.

Things to Consider When Planning Sections

What is the maximum size you are comfortable machine quilting? This is a personal decision, but most people are comfortable machine quilting a crib quilt, so that general size, between 36″ x 45″ and 45″ x 60″, is a logical target.

Does the weight factor affect your answer to the first question? It does for me. A flannel quilt is heavier than regular cotton. Cotton batting is heavier than polyester batting. The safety pins I use when layering are heavier than thread basting or spray basting. The heavier the piece that you are quilting, the harder it is to manipulate, the more likely you are to find smaller sections more satisfactory.

What is the complexity of the quilting you plan to do? Generally complex quilting, such as feathered wreath designs, will be more easily accomplished on smaller pieces. Less demanding quilting is perfect for larger pieces.

More specifically, what is your quilting plan? Planning the quilting is important when you start any quilt. It becomes even more important when quilting in sections, because the quilting plan also controls the way the sections can be joined. The key point to remember is that if you quilt to the edge of the fabric on both sections to be joined, finishing strips are usually required. Conversely, if one of the sections can be left without quilting for at least one inch from the edge, there are alternative joining methods.

How will the sections be assembled? While the methods in this book are not difficult, some take more time than others. Some assembly techniques add more bulk than others or require hand finishing.

All of these issues will influence your decisions. In Mix and Match Case Studies, Chapter 4, we will use an "issues and answers" process to look at many different questions and the solutions used. In Chapters 4 and 5, we'll also look at dividing quilts into diagonal rows, medallion units and less common shapes. In fact, planning the divisions will be discussed for every quilt shown in the book. My goal is that you will see ideas and methods here that you will apply to your own quilts.

Preparing the Quilt Top Sections

You may have heard the expression, "It will quilt out!" That is a little saying we quiltmakers use when we want to ignore a problem in the quilt top and we don't want to rip out a seam. It is true that some piecing irregularities can be disguised with careful quilting, but the reality is that most things don't "quilt out." Most problems are easier to correct as soon as possible. The alternative is to keep dealing with them every step of the way.

Check Section Sizes

Make sure sections match before layering for quilting. The number one rule for quilting in sections is to make sure all sections that will be sewn together after quilting have seams that match at intersections and in length. Before you begin layering, measure the sections or, better yet, pin them together, as if to seam them. If they don't match now, they won't match after they are quilted!

1. Measure the sections. It is very important to measure your quilt sections carefully and accurately. Assuming you have squared up each of the blocks, the quilt's sections will most likely match.

2. Make any adjustments necessary. If the length of the edges of the sections that are to be sewn together don't match, make any adjustments needed. If you don't correct it now, any discrepancy will be more of a problem when quilted.

3. Trim threads. A long thread that shows through the top of the quilt after quilting is very frustrating. While you are preparing the quilt sections for layering, clean up the back of the patchwork.

4. Mark quilting designs, if necessary. If you are planning any quilting that requires marking, it is better to do it before layering with batting and backing.

Preparing the Batting Sections

Batting choices are always personal, but there are a couple of things to consider when selecting batting for quilting in sections. Generally, polyester batting is less bulky than cotton batting in the seams where the sections are joined. Polyester can provide more loft if you are not planning on a lot of quilting.

Low-Batt Seams

Eliminate batting from seams by cutting the batting smaller and stitching or fusing it to the backing ⅜" from the seam edge before joining sections. This method is especially useful with cotton batting, see page 10.

Cut Large Pieces into Sections

One of the most frequently asked questions about quilting in sections is, "Does it take more batting to quilt in sections?" Just a little, but generally it is not necessary to buy a larger size packaged batt. You will simply have less scrap. For example, look at the layout for the Bed of Roses quilt. Lay out a full batt. Then arrange the quilt pieces on it as they will be arranged in the quilt, except allow a little bit extra on each side. Typically, you will still use the same size batt as you would for using traditional quilting methods.

Using quilt sections as a pattern for cutting batting sections

Create Large Sections from Scraps

Quilting in sections, especially blocks and strips, often allows you to use scraps of batting. If it is necessary to piece batting scraps, try the following technique.

Overlap the ends of the pieces slightly. Make a new wavy cut through both layers at one time to create matching edges. The wavy line is less likely than a straight cut to have any visible show-through:

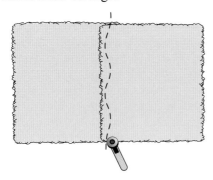

Remove the excess ends and butt the newly cut edges together. Center Fusible Tape over the cut and fuse sections together. (See Chapter 2, Low Fat Quilting.) If stitching the sections together, use the hand herringbone stitch shown below for an almost invisible result.

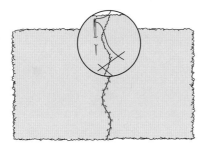

Some people recommend joining batting scraps with a machine zigzag stitch, but my experience is that it adds bulk, flattens the batting and distorts the batting.

Eliminating the Wrinkles

Regardless of which fiber or brand of batting you use, if it is packaged, it often holds wrinkles or creases. Most people recommend opening the package the day before you want to use it to let the batt relax. I don't think this is good enough. I actually prepare the batting one of two ways, neither of which is suitable for the new fusible battings! Both ways require completely unfolding the batt.

One option is to put the batting into the dryer with a couple of bath towels that have completed the spin dry cycle in the washer. Dry only for about 10 minutes before checking. You must be especially careful about the time if the batt is polyester. In fact, since dryer temperatures vary dramatically, you may want to try air dry only on polyester and see if that is adequate. Repeat for another 5 to 10 minutes if necessary. It should be light and fluffy and virtually all the wrinkles should be gone.

The second option is to use a steam iron and ironing board. Arrange the batting on the ironing board, cover with a single layer of cotton fabric and lightly run the steaming iron across the cotton fabric. Steam the entire area, move the batt and repeat. Keep repeating until you have gone over the entire batt.

Preparing the Backing Sections

Just as you can use scraps of batting, it is fun to use multiple pieces of fabric for the backing. On the quilts in this book, some backings coordinate with the front and some have no relationship to it at all. I often do some piecing and incorporate some of the leftover fabrics from the front of the quilt. Since I am machine quilting, I don't have to worry about the extra bulk the seams might add.

Layering the Sections

You will layer and baste in the same way you typically layer a crib quilt for machine quilting. If you are not experienced with layering, see page 67, Layering and Quilting in Sections. In fact, you may find unexpected savings in time during this step. First, because the pieces are manageable by one person, you don't have to wait for a friend or go to a special location with large tables to layer a quilt. Second, I have found I can successfully use the new timesaving spray adhesives for layering small pieces, but I'm still not comfortable using them to layer a big quilt.

Quilting

If the sections line up accurately before they are layered, are handled carefully during the layering process and are quilted in a similar fashion, they should match when joined. The more densely a section is quilted, the more likely it is to change size, so make sure the amount of quilting in the pieces is balanced.

Six Ways to Tame the Raw Edges

When people start thinking about quilting in sections, the first question is usually, "What do you do with all the raw edges?" You are probably thinking it just isn't possible to sew layered quilted sections together without having exposed messy-looking raw edges. You're almost right; it can't be done with a simple seam. However, there are six different ways discussed in this book for taming the raw edges of quilted sections. They are:

- The Four-Layer Seam, or Stitch and Flip; see Chapter 1, Border Control.

- Eliminating raw edges of sections by dividing only the batting, discussed in Chapter 2, Low-Fat Quilting.

- The five-layer seam, discussed in this chapter.

- The six-layer seam discussed in Chapter 1, Border Control, but reviewed here.

- Adding finishing strips, or the eight-layer seam.

- Creating an insert, or adding covering strips.

Read this section carefully to see how the way you quilt will affect the methods you can use to join sections. Don't be afraid to modify some of these methods or create entirely different techniques. For example, while I've never made a low-carb quilt where backing is brought to the front of sections and used for finishing, it certainly can be done.

As you read about these methods, think about quilts you have made or plan to make. Try to visualize using some of these techniques on your quilts.

Using the Four-Layer Seam
Because this method is most frequently used to add borders, it is discussed in Chapter 1, Border Control, page 11.

Eliminating Raw Edges of Sections by Dividing Only the Batting
See Chapter 2, Low-Fat Quilting, page 13.

Using the Five-Layer Seam As in the Texas Star
When quilting stops at least one inch from the seam line on one section, you can join the sections using a five-layer seam, which creates less bulk than assembling the sections with finishing strips.

The Texas Star, made in the "strippy" fashion and shown on page 30, is a perfect example of an appropriate use of a five-layer seam.

Twenty-one pieced Texas Star blocks are set with pieced triangular units to make three vertical panels, or strips. Two panels of appliquéd folk flowers separate the patchwork strips. All of these panels were layered and quilted individually before any quilt assembly was done. The quilting on the patchwork included in-the-ditch quilting that went off the edge of the patchwork. The quilting on the appliqué panels accented the curved lines of the appliqué and did not encroach on the edge of the panels. This makes the appliqué panels ideal for joining to the patchwork panel with the five-layer seam. This method is most neatly finished by hand, which takes more time than other seams.

1. Trim away excess batting and backing on all panels before beginning. Plan the visual order of the quilt's five center panels. Mark the top end of each panel.

2. Start with the center patchwork strip. With tops of both strips matching, lay one appliqué strip face down on the center patchwork strip. Pull the backing fabric on the appliqué strip away from the batting, shown below.

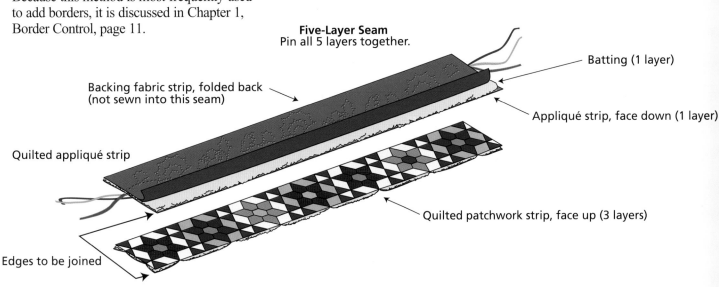

Five-Layer Seam
Pin all 5 layers together.

Backing fabric strip, folded back (not sewn into this seam)

Batting (1 layer)

Appliqué strip, face down (1 layer)

Quilted appliqué strip

Quilted patchwork strip, face up (3 layers)

Edges to be joined

3. With right sides together, pin the two panels together through the remaining five layers of fabric and batting.

4. Using a ¼″ seam allowance, stitch the five pinned layers together.

5. Trim away batting if it extends beyond the ¼″ seam allowance. To reduce excess bulk, you may also want to trim batting out of the seam allowance. Press the seam allowances toward the appliqué strip.

6. Press under ¼″ on the unstitched backing fabric. When the backing fabric of the appliqué strip is returned to a flat position, it should perfectly cover the seam line without pulling or gaping.

> Do not turn under more than ¼″ of fabric or the back will become smaller than the front of the quilt and create a bubble on the front!

7. Use your best hidden hand stitch to secure the folded edge of the backing of the appliqué strip. Let the visible stitching line be your guide and your anchor. Repeat with the appliqué border on the other side of the center strip.

With the three center strips joined, you can now add the outside strips of patchwork. Again, it is the backing of the appliqué sections that will be pulled away from the batting and not sewn into the seam.

Using the Six-Layer Seam As in the Texas Star

When most of the appliqué and buttonhole stitch was finished on the borders, but they were not quilted, the side borders were added using the six-layer seam method. This method can only be used when one section has no quilting.

> **Assembly Order for Quilt Borders with Blunt Corners**
> Add side borders first and then top and bottom borders. It will result in all four borders being similar in length. This is especially nice when you are cutting the borders on the lengthwise grain (see page 8).

1. Starting with either side of the quilt interior, position the appliquéd, but not quilted, border face down on the front of the quilt center and pin in place.

2. On the back of the quilt, pin the border backing and the quilt interior right sides together. Finally, add the border batting on either the front or the back. Pin these six layers together, shown below, with pins perpendicular to the raw edge, every 4″ to 6″.

3. Stitch all six layers together ¼″ from the edge.

4. Pull border, border backing and border batting away from the quilt's center. Press. Pin or baste to prepare the borders for quilting. In this quilt there is only one wide border.

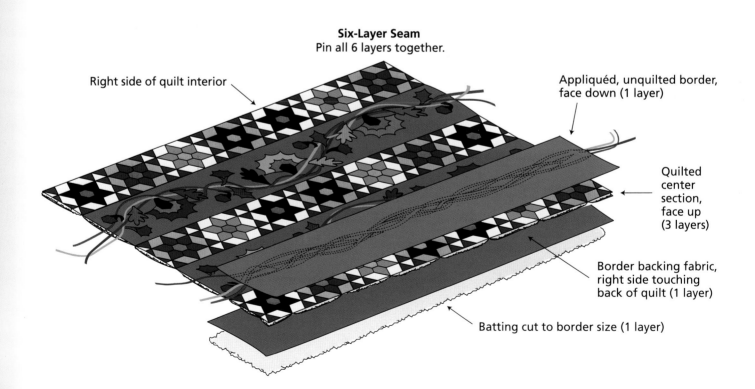

Six-Layer Seam
Pin all 6 layers together.

Right side of quilt interior

Appliquéd, unquilted border, face down (1 layer)

Quilted center section, face up (3 layers)

Border backing fabric, right side touching back of quilt (1 layer)

Batting cut to border size (1 layer)

Righthand border is ready to quilt.

Both borders are ready to quilt.

The illustration below is a cross-section view of how the border and batting pieces will look after the six-layer seam is made.

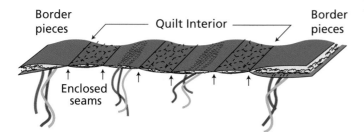

5. Repeat on opposite side, shown above, right.

6. The top and bottom borders are added in the same way.

See the finished Texas Star quilt on page 30. Can you tell it was quilted in sections? Only from the back!

Adding Finishing Strips
As in the Bed of Roses

Quilting adjoining sections all the way to their edges precludes using either the five- or six-layer seam method for joining them. An easy solution is finishing strips—a method that could be called the eight-layer seam. A finishing strip is a narrow folded strip of fabric that is sewn into the seam that joins the quilted sections. The strip is folded over to cover the raw seam allowance and a second stitching operation secures the loose edge on the back of the quilt. This can be by hand or with the machine blind hem stitch. It is a very simple solution, but will result in a bulkier finish than either the five- or six-layer seams.

1. The finishing strips are cut on the lengthwise grain, 1½" or 2" wide and approximately 2" longer than the lengths of the sections to be joined. Cut 1½" wide when finishing by hand and 2" wide when finishing with a machine blind hem stitch. Press the strips in half lengthwise, wrong sides together.

> Need to reduce bulk? Instead of cutting a 1½" finishing strip, folding it in half, and sewing two layers of fabric into the seam, use a 1" wide single layer strip. Fold under the raw edge when doing the hand finishing in step 5 below.

2. On the quilted sections, trim away any excess batting and backing to match the edge of the quilt top. In addition, on any corner that will be sewn into another seam with finishing strips, cut away a square of batting just big enough to eliminate batting from being caught in the seam.

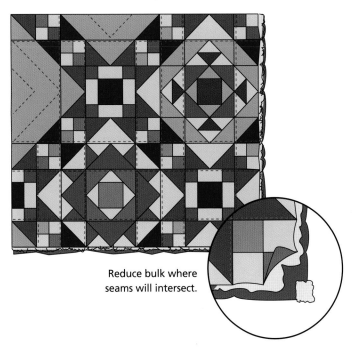

Reduce bulk where seams will intersect.

3. Layer two adjacent sections, right sides together. Then place a folded strip on the sections, aligning all raw edges. Pin both sections and the finishing strip together. Stitch ¼" from the raw edges through all eight layers.

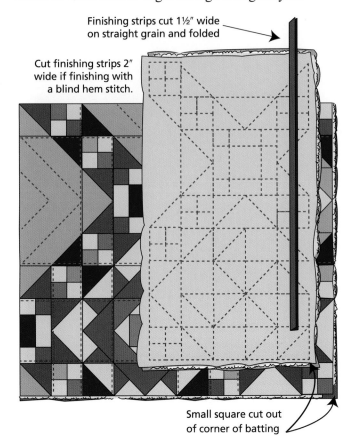

Finishing strips cut 1½" wide on straight grain and folded

Cut finishing strips 2" wide if finishing with a blind hem stitch.

Small square cut out of corner of batting

> Does it matter on which section the finishing strip is placed? Not usually. The strip will extend onto the side it was not laying on when the seam was sewn. It matters more in a quilt where you are quilting by the block than by the section (see Picnic Basket, page 62).

4. To reduce bulk, you can trim away some of the batting in the seam allowance. If the panels are pulled firmly over your knee, the seam opens up and it is easy to trim away the excess batting between the layers of fabric. It should not be necessary to cut away fabric.

5. After trimming the batting, press the strip to the side so that it covers all the raw edges. Hand stitch the folded edge in place with a hidden stitch. If you don't mind a machine stitch showing on the finishing strip, this step can be done with your machine blind hem stitch. (See your machine manual for blind hem stitch instructions.) Turn quilt back carefully so hem stitch catches only the quilt backing.

Creating an Insert
Or Using Covering Strips

This is a slightly modified version of a technique that I learned from Barb Cleaver. She is a Brisbane, Australia, quilter who has made clever use of Quilt-As-You-Sew techniques and has been including quilting in sections in her designs for years. This particular technique, which she calls "covering strips," is perfect for quilt blocks or sections that you would like to join with sashing. In fact, the method results in an insert of some width on both the front and back of your quilt. You can see on page 42 that Barb has beautifully worked the covering strips into her quilt called Sparkling Diamonds.

Units are quilted before being assembled into a quilt top; think of each square in our diagrams as a section. In the sample illustrated, some sections have batting and backing extending on two sides, some on four sides, and corner blocks are trimmed clean, with no batting extending. Barb finds it easier to make batting and backing pieces the same size when cutting, even though some of the backing fabric is trimmed away to reduce bulk after the covering strips are sewn in place.

> Read these instructions before quilting your units and refer to the illustrations as needed. To adapt this technique to other block arrangements, just remember: when joining two sections with a covering strip, batting and backing slightly wider than the covering strip must extend from one of them. The edge of the second unit is clean cut.

The first thing you must do is decide what width the covering strips will be and add ½″ for seam allowances. That will determine the extra width to allow when cutting batting and backing pieces. Don't forget to determine how many sides of each section will need the extra width. This is where planning pays off. Look at Row 1 in the previous illustration. In Row 1, Sections A and B alternate, beginning and ending with A. In Row 2, Sections C and D alternate. In the examples shown, Rows 1 and 2 alternate, and the quilt ends with a Row 1.

Making the Rows

1. Lay covering strips on both sides of Section B on the front, right sides together. Stitch in place using a ¼″ seam.

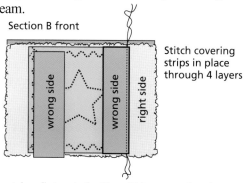

Section B front

Stitch covering strips in place through 4 layers

2. Press strips flat onto batting. Trim away batting and backing to match. Lift and trim away more backing only, to reduce bulk. Don't trim closer than ¼″ from seam.

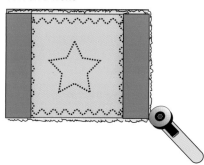

Section B front

3. Place Section A on top of Section B, lining up the edge of the quilted unit with the edge of the covering strip and batting.

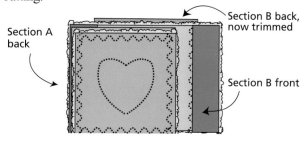

Section A back

Section B back, now trimmed

Section B front

Add another covering strip on the top, right sides together. Stitch through all six layers with a ¼″ seam allowance.

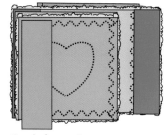

Ready for sewing

Row 1 (First and last row)

Section A
4 clean edges

Section B
sides have batting

Section A
4 clean edges

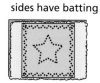

Row 2 (alternate Rows 1 and 2 for quilt interior)

Section C
top and bottom
have batting

Section D
4 edges have batting

Section C
top and bottom
have batting

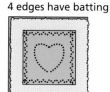

4. The covering strip on the front is caught in seams on both sides. The covering strip on the back is caught on one edge only.

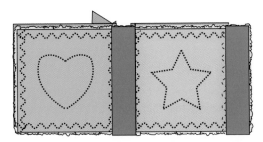

5. On the free edge of the covering strip, carefully press under exactly ¼″. Use the machine stitching on the back of Section B as a guide and stitch the covering strip in place by hand.

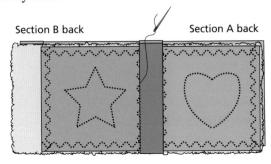

Section B back   Section A back

6. Turn this section over and add the next Section A in the same manner.

Section A/B front

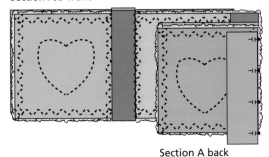

Section A back

Continue alternating sections, if needed, to complete Row 1.

7. Assemble Row 2 in the same manner, alternating Sections C and D.

Joining the Rows

1. Cut long covering strips the same width as the strips between the sections in the rows. Place one strip right side down on both long sides of Row 2. Pin and stitch in place ¼″ from the edge.

Row 2 front

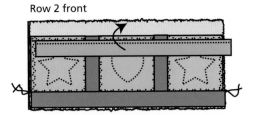

2. Open and press stitched covering strips onto batting. Trim batting to match and trim backing to just ¼″ to ½″ beyond the stitching line.

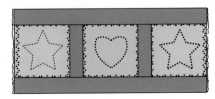

3. Pin Row 1 and a covering strip in place as shown and stitch.

Row 2 front   Row 1 back

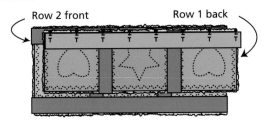

4. Open and hand finish back covering strip as when joining sections.

Continue making and joining rows until the quilt interior is your desired size. Borders could be added using either the five- or six-layer seam method. See Chapter 6 for information on bindings.

Front

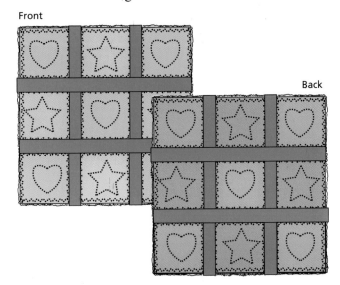

Back

Chapter 4

Mix and Match Case Studies

What do the quilts in this book have in common? You can't tell from the front. You might have a hard time telling from the back, but they were all quilted in easy-to-handle low-carb quilting sections. These quilts were made for other projects, not specifically for this book, but all of them were quilted in sections because it made sense. Now it makes sense to bring all of these quilts together and include the methods and the decision making processes in one book.

As you thumb through this chapter, you will see three headings for each quilt. Under Issues and Answers, you will find condensed questions or issues about the quilt and, side-by-side, our answers or solutions. Commentary will include things like background information, more detail, resources, et cetera.

Remember—planning ahead is the key to success when quilting in sections.

If you fail to plan ahead, don't forget there is always Low-Fat Quilting, discussed in Chapter 2, as a fall-back position. In this book, only the Rose Garden Hidden Stars sampler was quilted using that method.

For the most flexibility in your quiltmaking, try to think about all the methods for quilting in sections and remember that most can be adapted to any quilt. Then it is easy to mix and match methods.

Problem solving is part of the planning process.

In some cases, pictures were taken while the quilt was in progress, with the hope it would make visualizing the concept much easier.

Many of the quilts are full-size Queen/Double bed quilts. When I show them at guild meetings or classes, people always exclaim about the size. I just remind them that a quilt that actually fits a bed is big—and that is the number one reason to consider quilting it in sections.

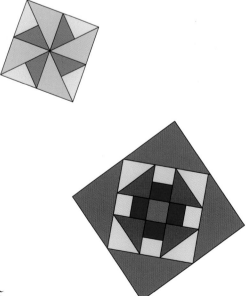

Case Study: Bed of Roses

Approximate Finished Size: 80″ x 104″ *(*203.2 cm x 264.2 cm)

Commentary

Bed of Roses is a straight set quilt featuring 16″ blocks and fairly wide borders. You may not be able to tell from the picture that Bed of Roses is a flannel quilt. Because it was also going to be backed with flannel, it would be heavier than a regular cotton quilt.

Issues	Answers
1. This will be a large flannel quilt with large blocks, wide borders and flannel backing.	**1.** Divide the quilt in sections to quilt, especially since the weight of a flannel back is included.
2. If quilted in sections, planned quilt-in-the-ditch quilting will go across the edges of pieces.	**2.** Sections with quilting across the edge will require finishing strips to join the sections. Minimize the number of sections and at the same time reduce the risk of long straight seams not matching.
3. There are three borders. Should they be joined before adding to the quilt?	**3.** Borders that are joined before being added to a quilt require mitered corners and I try to avoid them when quilting in sections. Instead, add the first border and the border batting and backing pieces using the six-layer seam. Add subsequent borders using the stitch and flip technique (page 10).

In Chapter 1, we discussed ways to control the bulk of the quilt with simple changes to how borders are added. With the extra weight of flannel, quilting the interior and adding borders later would be a good idea for Bed of Roses, but that alone would not provide enough relief from the weight of the quilt while quilting. It would surely be an ideal candidate for dividing the interior of the quilt and quilting in sections.

What is a good way to divide the quilt? Same-size quarters of the quilt would have required breaking some of the blocks into sections and some pieces into smaller pieces. That option is not desirable. Dividing the block creates the opportunity to turn a section the wrong way and dividing a piece adds extra bulk. The quilt could have been divided into four sections that would be sewn together with short horizontal seams and a long straight vertical seam. Occasionally, when machine quilting, there is a slight

distortion at the edge of a section, either because it never was the right size or it stretched during quilting. If the patchwork seams don't line up perfectly, uneven seams are much more apparent in a long straight seam, below left, than in a broken line, below right. So we chose to divide the quilt top with a broken vertical line.

The actual section sizes are shown in the small diagram. All five pieces are a size that is easy for most people to machine quilt.

The quilt interior could have been divided into two long sections: one, two blocks wide and the length of the quilt and one, three blocks wide.

36" x 40"	24" x 36"

	12" x 40"
24" x 52"	40" x 40"

The sections would have been quite manageable to quilt, but the same problem of one long joining seam would exist.

Offsetting some of the finishing seams also made the back of the quilt much more attractive. I had several pieces of leftover flannel that were perfect for section backing fabrics. Some of the backing sections were actually pieced to make it even more interesting. Contrasting and pieced finishing strips added to the fun of the back of this quilt.

This is just one example of planning the sections. My decisions are not right or wrong, they are just my choice for this quilt. The pictures of the divided quilt from the front and of the finished quilt from the back will help you see the

sections in which it was quilted. After the quilt interior was completed, the first border was added using the six-layer seam method. It is easy to see the border backing strips when you look at the back of the quilt. You can also see that the side borders were added first, and then the top and bottom. Subsequent borders were added using the stitch and flip technique.

Complete instructions for making the Bed of Roses are available in the pattern Bed of Roses/Downhill Dreamer, *Product #30058 from Michell Marketing, Inc., or ask at your favorite quilt shop. The pattern also includes instructions for a twin size sampler and tips on pillow case construction.*

Case Study: Stippled Postage Stamp Basket

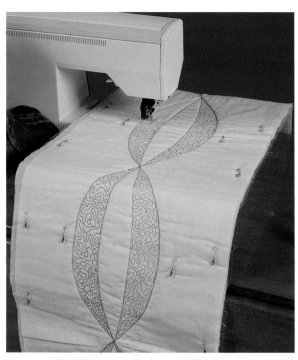

Approximate Finished Size:
85" x 99" (215.9 cm x 251.5 cm)

Commentary

In the Stippled Postage Stamp Basket, twenty blocks were stippled and quilted through the top, batting and backing using colored thread. Because quilting did not extend to the edge of the blocks, they could be joined into rows with five-layer seams.

When the interior of the quilt was completed, accurate measurements were taken and the borders were cut, marked and quilted individually. Again, the color of the thread used for stippling created the design.

Look closely and you can tell there is an acrylic surround around the open arm of the sewing machine that makes the sewing area level. Ours is the Sew Steady Portable Table from Dream World Northwest (see Resources, page 72).

Complete directions and pattern for the Stippled Postage Stamp Basket quilt are available in Weekend Basket Quilts *by Marti Michell, published by American School of Needlework, ASN Publishing, 1993 (now out of print).*

Issues	Answers
1. The entire design will be created with machine stipple quilting—very difficult to do on a whole cloth quilt.	**1.** Instead, work in sections: 20 individual blocks and four borders will be easiest.
2. Units will require joining.	**2.** Neither the blocks nor the border have quilting to the edge, so they can all be joined with five-layer seam method. It may be easier to use finishing strips when rows of blocks are joined.
3. The quilting design in the border is continuous, but the border would be added in sections—how?	**3.** The border is designed with blunt corners so that the sections join at a place with virtually no quilting.

Case Study: Texas Star

Approximate Finished Size: 82½″ x 114″ (209.6 cm x 289.6 cm)

Issues	Answers
1. This will be a very large quilt, 82½″ by 114″.	**1.** Divide the quilt into sections for quilting.
2. The quilt is a strippy style design.	**2.** Perfect! The strips provide a natural division. Use different fabrics for the backing pieces and create an interesting strippy back, too.
3. What about quilting?	**3.** The interior strips should all be quilted individually for ease in handling,
4. How would the strips be joined?	**4.** Because the patchwork would be quilted to the edge and the appliqué strips would not, it would be possible to use five-layer seams to join the inner sections.
5. Will the continuous appliqué design on the border cause problems?	**5.** Most of the appliqué could be completed on the borders before adding them to the quilt interior. However, the appliqué design at the corners would need to be completed after the borders were added. The general complexity of the borders made us decide to quilt them after they were added. By not quilting the borders before they were added, it would be possible to add them with the six-layer seam, which would mean no handwork or finishing strips would be needed.

Commentary

When last we saw the Texas Star quilt there were only two borders added; see diagrams on page 21. The quilt was used as an example of controlling raw edges with both five- and six-layer seams.

In reality, the interior appliqué strips, shown with five-layer seams, could be added to the center patchwork panel before quilting using the six-layer seam method. It would mean quilting the appliqué strips when the total center section is about 40 inches wide by 85 inches long. However, you would only be quilting on 14 inches of width and all of the rest of the quilt would be to the left of the needle. You might prefer to quilt in that fashion and avoid the handwork. That is the kind of question to which each quiltmaker must supply his or her own answer.

Subsequently, the top and bottom borders were also added using the six-layer seam. The borders were quilted after they were added to the quilt interior. The quilt was big and bulky, but because all of the final quilting on the borders took place within 14 inches of the edge of the quilt, it was not necessary to roll the bulk of the quilt and make it fit through the machine opening.

It would have been possible to quilt these borders and then add them, but the vine design is continuous around the corners and, either way, parts of the vine had to be left incomplete while borders were added. Our decision

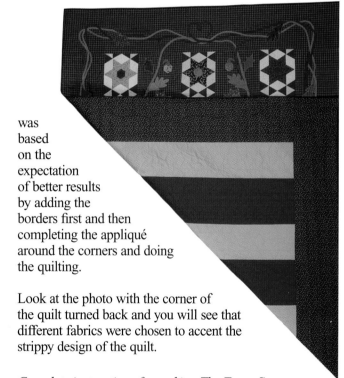

was based on the expectation of better results by adding the borders first and then completing the appliqué around the corners and doing the quilting.

Look at the photo with the corner of the quilt turned back and you will see that different fabrics were chosen to accent the strippy design of the quilt.

Complete instructions for making The Texas Star are available in the pattern Texas Gardens, *Product #8969 from Michell Marketing, Inc., or ask at your favorite quilt shop. The pattern also includes the same basic design in a size small enough to quilt in one piece, 35¼″ by 42½″.*

Case Study: Cabin by the Lake

Approximate Finished Size: 86″ x 103″ (218.4 cm x 261.6 cm)

Commentary

This large sampler quilt is a flannel quilt with a flannel back; in other words, this quilt is heavier than the average quilt. Both the bulk of the flannel and the precision necessary for the mitered corner meant that adding completely separate border sections was not a favorable option for reducing the actual size of the unit to be quilted.

Instead, we decided to quilt the center section first, then add borders using the four-layer seam or stitch and flip technique. The result is that the folded and pinned section is much smaller and lighter than if the four borders were already sewn on.

After the center is quilted, one side is released and a border is added using the four-layer seam. It is smoothed into place and pinned. Now the border can be quilted, but the amount of quilt that must be manipulated through the opening is limited to the width of the border. Everything else is to the left of the needle. See the photo of the quilt with the last border being added, page 33.

Issues	Answers
1. This is a large flannel quilt, 86″ by 103″, with a flannel back—heavy!	**1.** Thermore™ by Hobbs, a very lightweight polyester batting was chosen to reduce both bulk and weight.
2. Extra seams can add even more bulk and weight.	**2.** In order to eliminate any extra seams, the batting and backing was cut to the finished size needed for the complete quilt.
3. The quilt top could easily be divided into one center medallion area and four borders. See illustrations on the next page.	**3.** The interior of the sampler with the narrow first border added (51½″ by 68½″) was centered on the full-size batting and backing and layered and basted as normal. Then, the area with exposed batting was folded and pinned to reduce the size of the area that must be manipulated through the machine. The new size is just a little larger than the center section. (See The Four-Layer Seam, page 11.)
4. Mitered corner precision is necessary when adding the pieced borders.	**4.** This corner is actually more easily completed with a mock miter; that is hand stitching from the top, like appliquéing one border edge to the next.

In the illustration at right, the top and bottom borders are in place. The left side border is stitched and ready to be flipped onto the batting and backing. The righthand border is pieced and ready to add for quilting.

In the photograph of the actual quilt, below, three borders are in position for quilting and the fourth has been stitched in place. The back of the fabric and the batting at the seamline almost match, making it hard to see, but the enlarged section should help.

Cabin by the Lake was a design developed for a Maywood Studio "Not So Block of the Month" program. The fabric and the pattern are no longer available.

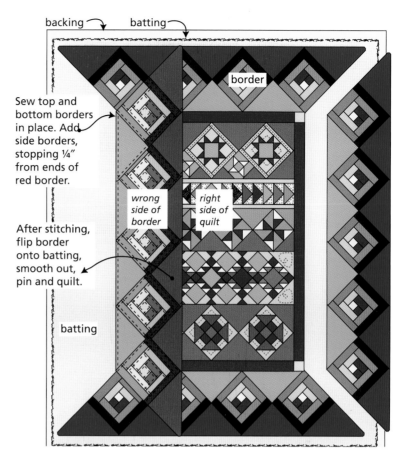

backing

batting

border

Sew top and bottom borders in place. Add side borders, stopping ¼" from ends of red border.

wrong side of border

right side of quilt

After stitching, flip border onto batting, smooth out, pin and quilt.

batting

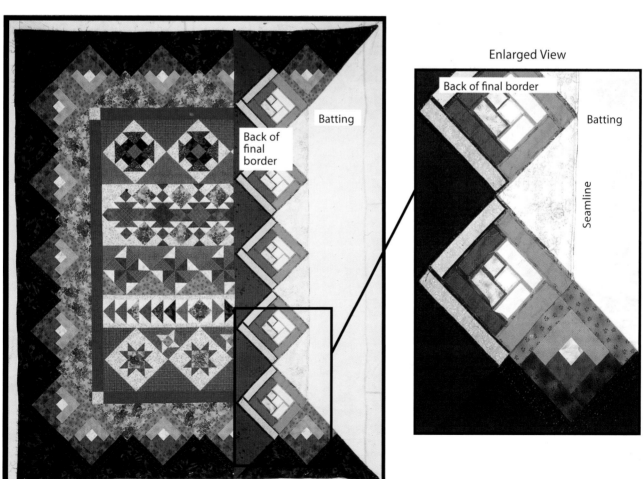

Batting

Back of final border

Enlarged View

Back of final border

Batting

Seamline

Case Study: The Feathered Heart Wallhanging

Approximate Finished Size: 31″ (78.7 cm) square

The Feathered Heart Wallhanging pattern was included in Marti's book, Successful Machine Quilting, *Meredith Press, 1995, now out of print but possibly available at your library and sometimes spotted on eBay™.*

Commentary

Most of the emphasis in this book has been on the advantages of quilting bed-size quilts in small sections. This quilt is a perfect example of why you would want to quilt small quilts in sections. It was so much easier to quilt all of the feather quilting in five small sections than in one large piece.

After the excess batting and backing on the five sections was trimmed away, the pieces were ready to join. Because the quilting did not cross the edge of any piece, five-layer seams could be used to join all sections. The pattern used included drawn seam lines that were carefully matched as two opposite corner sections were added to the center square. The backing for the square was the layer that was not sewn into any seam. The other two corners were carefully positioned in place and actually basted so that the quilt could be examined from the front to make sure the feathered quilting design in the borders were properly aligned. Finally, the batting was trimmed out of the seam and the backing fabric for the square turned under so the folded edge was directly on top of the seam line and stitched in place.

Now, imagine this same quilt layout as a medallion center big enough for a queen-size bed. Then imagine adding wide borders. Wouldn't you be glad to quilt that in nine sections?

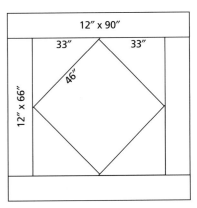

Issues	Answers
1. Entire design includes feather quilting.	1. Take advantage of the natural divisions (center square and four corners) to quilt in sections for much easier manipulation.
2. How will the pieces be joined?	2. All four corner sections can be added using a five-layer seam. Crucial for doing this successfully is that, in all four seams, the backing fabric on the center square must be the layer that is not sewn into the seam.
3. Border design must be aligned perfectly when pieces are joined.	3. Basting seams is a rarity for me, but I would recommend basting the third and fourth corners in place to make sure the quilting design and edges line up properly.

Case Study: Rose Garden Express

Approximate Finished Size: 80″ x 100″
(203.2 cm x 254 cm)

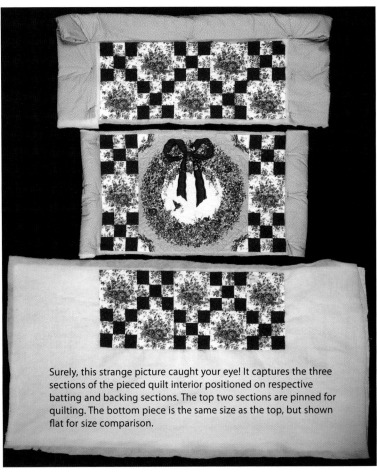

Surely, this strange picture caught your eye! It captures the three sections of the pieced quilt interior positioned on respective batting and backing sections. The top two sections are pinned for quilting. The bottom piece is the same size as the top, but shown flat for size comparison.

Commentary

When the Rose Garden fabric by **From Marti Michell** and Maywood Studio was introduced in five different colors, we wanted to make several quilts to show off the printed wreath panel and garland in a hurry. With the first color combination, I missed a very easy way to divide the quilt. One day, looking at the picture, the proverbial light bulb went on and I realized how easy it would be to quilt the next version in sections. Backing and batting are typically calculated by adding at least 4″ to both dimensions of the finished size of the quilt top. Add an additional 4″ to the length to allow for the horizontal division in this method. The quilt is divided into almost equal thirds.

Issues	Answers
1. This is a full-size bed quilt with an elaborate central printed panel surrounded by patchwork and plain alternate blocks. It is imperative that a seam does not run across the beautiful garland border pieces.	**1.** The pieced interior sections were positioned, layered and pinned in place. Excess batting and backing pieces were rolled up and pinned in place to reduce the size of each piece for quilting. The three sections could be assembled with a five-layer seam, assuming quilting on the center section does not extend within an inch of the edge. If it does, use finishing strips.
2. The quilt batting and backing will be full size when the three sections are joined. It is ready for the borders. There are mitered corners on the first border.	**2.** Add the mitered print border in the same way as the pieced Log Cabin border of Cabin by the Lake. Finish mitered corners by hand.
3. There are three additional borders.	**3.** The borders can be added stitch and flip one at a time, or joined and added as a unit and then quilted. All of the work for adding borders will take place within 18″ of the edge.

Case Study: A Nine Patch Trip Around the World

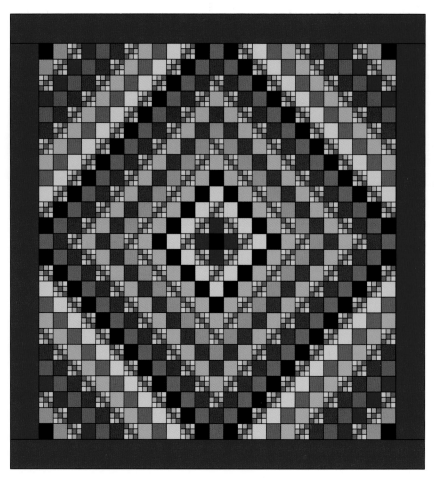

Approximate Finished Size: 87″ (221 cm) square

Commentary

At first glance, you might think the easiest way to quilt this Trip Around the World in sections would be to divide the quilt into quarters. However, because the interior of this quilt has an odd number of squares, the quilt cannot be divided into four exactly equal quarters. So, the quilt interior was divided roughly into quarters and measured. The border width and at least an additional 2″ are added on two adjoining sides. Using those measurements, cut four individual backing and batting sections.

The Trip Around the World interior sections are not centered on the batting and backing, but positioned in one corner. The extended edges of the batting and backing are rolled up and pinned as shown in the illustration. This is done to reduce the size and cover the batting to eliminate catching batting in the presser foot or on dry skin. The borders are added using the stitch and flip method after the quilted sections are joined.

Issues	Answers
1. This is a big quilt, 87″ square, with machine guided quilting in the ditch and wide borders.	**1.** To maintain the integrity of the borders, divide the interior patchwork section and the batting and backing, allowing for the wide borders. Quilt the four sections and join with finishing strips, assuming the quilting went to the edge.
2. If the border pieces are included with the patchwork, there would be unsightly seamlines just off center in each border.	**2.** Add the borders using the stitch and flip method after the sections are assembled.

After the quilting is completed, remove the pins to release the rolled edges. Assuming the quilting went to two edges of each quadrant, the easiest way to join the sections is with the use of finishing strips; see details on page 22. Finally, add the borders using the four-layer seam, shown on page 11. Add sides first, then the top and bottom borders. It will be easy to add any additional quilting to the wide border because the area you need to quilt is only 6″ wide. The rest of the quilt is to the left the needle.

A Nine Patch Trip Around the World was first shown in 101 Nine Patch Quilt*s by Marti Michell, published by ASN Publishing, 2000.*

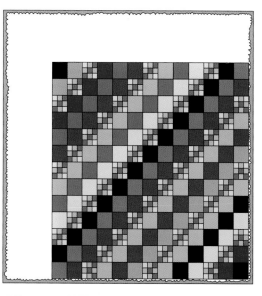
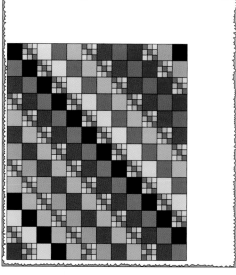
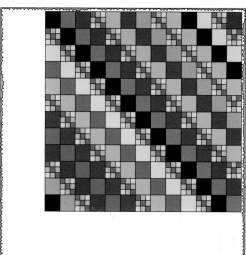
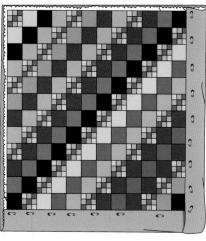

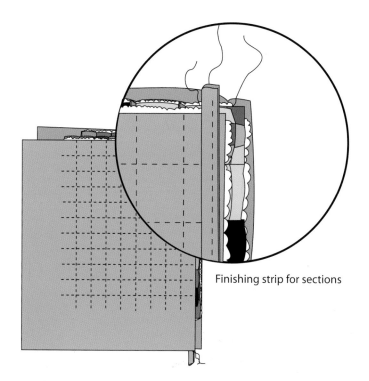

Finishing strip for sections

Illustration shows hand stitched finish. This can also be done using the blind hem stitch feature of your sewing machine.

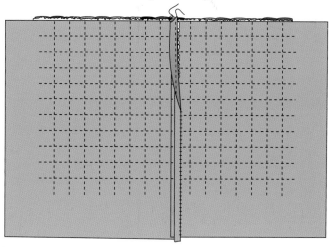

37

Case Study: Vintage Dresden Plate

Approximate Finished Size: 80¾″ x 102½″ (205.1 cm x 260.4 cm)

Issues	Answers
1. This will be a very large quilt, 80¾″ by 102½″.	**1.** Obviously, this is a candidate for dividing in sections, but it will be unusual. The interior of the quilt can be divided diagonally, but all seams do not go to the edge of the quilt.
2. It has a diagonal set center and straight borders. No seams go entirely across the quilt, edge to edge.	**2.** Batting and backing will be cut into diagonal sections, with enough extra allowed at the ends of each section to accommodate both of the stitch-and-flip borders.
3. Somewhat intricate quilting is planned.	**3.** Intricate quilting requires maneuverability. Smaller sections accommodate that need. Even though intricate quilting is planned, it will not go to the edge of the blocks. The blocks can be assembled with a five-layer seam and no finishing strips.
4. Cotton batting will be used.	**4.** Cotton batting creates more bulk when included in a seam than polyester batting, so it is usually desirable to avoid including it in seams. After the diagonal rows (including the excess batting and backing) are joined, the borders will be added using the stitch and flip technique, to eliminate extra batting in the border seams.

Commentary

In Chapter 5, there are instructions for four quilts, including Not Such Hard Times. It is a diagonal set quilt with alternating unpieced blocks. Please look at the photo on page 53 that shows the straightforward method for dividing that quilt top into five sections for quilting. It can be easily divided because the seams go from one edge of the quilt to the other.

Vintage Dresden Plate is also a diagonal set quilt, but it is considerably more complicated to finish in sections. It is a perfect example of why it is important to plan ahead. Because there are not continuous diagonal seams all across the quilt, it was necessary to add both the pieced border and the blue border after the interior quilting was done and the sections were sewn together. The illustration shows the seven sections in the interior of the quilt.

Several similar fabrics were selected for the backing of the sections, making the back subtle but very pretty.

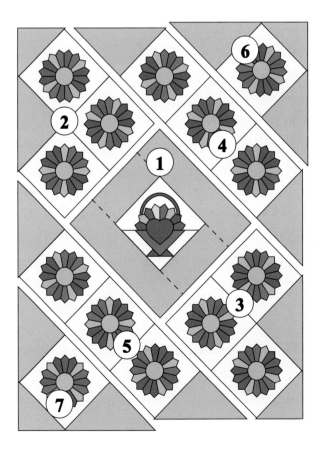

This is one of the quilts we were able to photograph in progress. In the first photograph, four sections have been quilted and three are ready for batting and backing to be added. In the second photograph, the sections have been assembled and three of the sawtooth borders have been added. The other borders are hanging on the back of the chair.

Look at the white batting in the pictures. I used cotton batting in this quilt and didn't want extra bulk in the seams. So instead of adding the borders with a six-layer seam, I extended the batting and backing and joined the sections using a four-layer seam. By including the extra backing fabric and the batting for the borders that were to be added, both the pieced border and the blue border could be added with a four-layer seam after the quilted units were put together.

Complete instructions for making Vintage Dresden Plate are available in the pattern Dresden Plate Homecoming, *Product #30086, from Michell Marketing, Inc. The pattern also includes a wallhanging and a miniature version of Vintage Dresden Plate (33½" by 42"), both small enough to quilt in one piece.* **From Marti Michell** *acrylic templates for rotary cutting Dresden Plate petals are also available, Product #8965. Ask for* **From Marti Michell** *products at your favorite quilt shop.*

40

Case Study: Some Enchanted Evening

Approximate Finished Size: 85″ x 102″ (215.9 cm x 259.1 cm)

Issues	Answers
1. This is a very large quilt, 85″ x 102″.	**1.** The quilt logically breaks into five pieces.
2. There are large alternate blocks with no piecing. They invite more intricate quilting.	**2.** The sections should be small enough that intricate free-motion quilting will be very easy to accomplish. How the sections are joined will depend on the quilting. If quilting goes into the seam allowance, use finishing strips to join sections.
3. The border of the quilt is really created with pieced blocks. The center of the quilt design breaks into the borders on the sides. There is no separate border.	**3.** When the quilt sections are joined, the quilt is complete and ready for binding.

Commentary

This quilt was designed as a "Not So Block of the Month" program for Maywood Studio. Because the large floral had a very "decorator look," the quilt was planned with large pieces and simple construction techniques. Since the simplicity of the quilt could be expected to appeal to beginners, it also seemed ideal to show how to quilt in sections.

If you choose minimal quilting, rather than elaborate quilting, the middle section can be quilted in one piece rather than three.

Finishing strips cut 1½″ wide on straight grain and folded in half if finishing by hand. Cut 2″ wide if finishing with a machine blind hem stitch.

*Small square cut out of corner of batting

Case Study: Sparkling Diamonds

Australian quilt artist Barb Cleaver is well known for her clever use of Quilt-As-You-Sew methods, which she used to make four diamond-shaped Log Cabin blocks for this quilt. She joined them and the other sections of her quilt using her Covering Strips method, which is detailed on pages 23 and 24. The contrasting covering strip becomes an important design line in the quilt.

This guest appearance of Barb's quilt resulted after Marti and Barb shared ideas while both were teaching at a conference in Australia. Special thanks go to Barb for generously sharing her covering strips technique.

Approximate Finished Size: 36″ x 48″ (91.4 cm x 122 cm)

Case Study: Shades of Baltimore ~ Winter

Approximate Finished Size: 45″ (114.3 cm) square

1. Position center medallion on batting and backing and quilt.

2. Add side blocks, then the top and bottom rows, using the stitch and flip method.

3. Add borders with six-layer seam.

Issues	Answers
1. Because some of the machine-guided buttonhole stitch was also doing the quilting, maneuverability was crucial.	1. Working in sections improves maneuverability.
2. Cotton batting provided the density desired for this wallhanging but is bulky in the six-layer seam planned for the borders.	2. Eliminate batting from seams by fusing it or stitching it to the backing ⅜″ from the edge of the backing. (See page 10.) Trim batting out of seam allowances before joining the sections. This is especially helpful with cotton batting.

Commentary

This is a relatively small wall quilt with fused appliqué designs. The edges of the fused pieces are finished with a machine buttonhole stitch. Because the buttonhole stitch is machine guided and not free-motion, it requires maneuverability of the quilt. In fact, many motifs required stitching in a complete circle.

On each block, most of the buttonhole work was done before assembling the quilt. However, the easiest section of each block was left to buttonhole stitch after layering the sections with batting and backing. That meant the quilting was completed at the same time. It also meant that quilting in sections from the center out would be very desirable.

Shades of Baltimore – Winter *instructions are available in pattern or kit form from Shades Textiles, www. shadestextiles.co. There are three additional quilt designs in the series, one for each season of the year.*

Case Study: Rose Wreath Appliqué

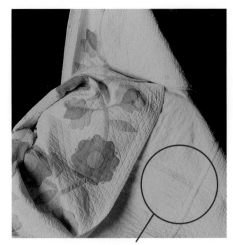

Finishing strips on quilt that was machine quilted in sections around 1875.

Approximate Finished Size: 64" x 80"
(162.6 cm x 203.2 cm)

Issues	Answers
1. How can a quiltmaker in 1875 with a brand new treadle sewing machine make sure everyone in town is aware of that fact?	**1.** She could machine quilt the hand appliquéd top she has recently finished.
2. The quilt seems too big to roll and squeeze through the small opening in the machine.	**2.** She probably thought, "Why not quilt it in five rows, and then put the rows together?" As the old saying goes, the rest is history!

Commentary

You may have noticed that most of the quilts discussed so far have been patchwork. In fact, because appliqué blocks can often be joined with a five-layer seam, they are usually easier to quilt in sections and join.

Also, up to now, most of the quilts shown were quilted in my studio. The techniques were developed to solve the problems we encountered while quilting full-size bed quilts on a regular domestic sewing machine.

This antique quilt is being shared to prove there is nothing new! When I started using and teaching quilting in sections with finishing strips, I had never seen the method, however, at least one quiltmaker used the same technique at a much earlier time.

Even though solid color quilts are difficult to date, it is thought the beautiful appliqué could have been completed as early as 1865–1870. It is also a relatively common belief among quilt researchers that the recipient of an early sewing machine might quilt by machine to "show off" the fact that she owned a sewing machine. As both an antique quilt collector and a proponent of machine quilting in sections, I was thrilled to purchase this very early example of machine quilting in sections.

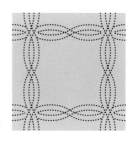

Chapter 5

Machine Quilting in Sections
Step by Step

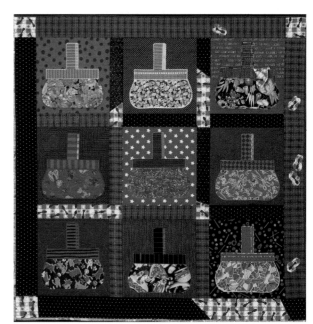

World Without End

Approximate Finished Size: 80½″ x 100½″ (204.5 cm x 255.3 cm)

Issues	Answers
1. This will be a very traditional 48-block patchwork quilt with plain borders.	**1.** Easily broken down into 48 individual blocks, but there is no need to work that small. Instead, 12 sections of four blocks were chosen as a nice compromise between a reasonable size for quilting and the extra work required for finishing strips.
2. Block sections will need to be joined and then borders will need to be added.	**2.** Join sections with finishing strips. Add first borders with six-layer seam and subsequent borders stitch and flip style (pages 9 and 10).

FINISHED SIZES

Queen/Double Quilt Size: 80½" x 100½"
  (204.5 cm x 255.3 cm)
Block Size: 10" (25.4 cm) square

MATERIALS REQUIRED

Fat quarter yard (18" x 22") each of
  16 assorted light background fabrics
Assorted scraps of medium to dark print fabrics
  totaling 1¾ yards (minimum size 6" x 8")
Assorted scraps of medium to dark accent fabrics
  totaling 1⅜ yards (minimum size 4" x 12")
⅞ yard of light fabric for first border
¾ yard of medium to dark fabric for second border
1½ yards of light fabric for third border
¾ yard of fabric for French-fold binding
6 yards total of fabric for backing; one fabric or several
Appropriate size packaged batting or scraps
Perfect Patchwork Templates Set Q. If you are a dedicated
  From MARTI MICHELL Perfect Patchwork Template user,
  Set Q, Triangle #94 and Square #93 will be perfect for all
  the smaller pieces in the World Without End quilt and Set
  T, Triangle #103 for the large triangles.

Selecting the Fabric

Over 100 different fabrics were used in making the 48
World Without End blocks. While each block has a different
combination of light, medium and dark fabrics, some of
the background fabrics are used in more than one block.
The large triangles in each block are generally medium- to
dark-colored large prints; the small triangles are medium to
dark accent fabrics; and the background fabric is always a
light print. Sets of four blocks, with medium accent fabrics
from the same color family, are combined to make 12 units
that are quilted individually.

Cutting the Fabric

For each of the 48 World Without End blocks, cut 2 large
A Triangles from the "theme" print, 6 small #94 accent
triangles, 10 small #94 background triangles and 4 small
#93 squares. In order to keep matching sets of pieces
together, it is recommended that you cut and assemble
blocks individually or just a few at a time.

When pieces that are to be sewn together are the
same size and can be cut together, layer fabrics
right sides together, then cut strips and in this case,
triangles. Keep the pieces layered so they are ready to
begin sewing. This is appropriate for triangle #94 in
the World Without End block.

Making the Block

The blocks are constructed in sub-units. Complete the
following steps for each block.

1. Use chain piecing to join pairs of accent and
background #94 Triangles. Make six half-square
triangle units for each block. Press the seam
allowance toward the dark fabric.
Make 6

2. Make four rectangles by chain piecing
four of the half-square triangles to a
matching Square #93. Be sure that all of
the units are in the same orientation as
you sew.
Make 4

3. For each block, join four units made in step 2, as shown.

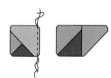

4. Make pieced triangles by adding a matching Triangle
94 to two adjacent sides of the remaining half-square
triangle units.

Make 2

5. Add a contrasting Triangle A to the pieced triangles
from step 4.

6. Join two units from step 3
and two from step 5
to complete each block.
Each of the 48 blocks
should measure 10½"
square, including seam
allowances.

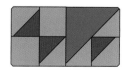

Assembling the Quilting Units

Lay the blocks out, rotating to obtain the proper position, and join sets of four blocks together into the 12 quilting units. Each unit should measure 20½" square, including seam allowances. Cut batting and backing pieces and layer each unit for quilting. This is a great chance to use some assorted fabrics you already own for the backing pieces. After quilting, join the blocks into four horizontal rows of three units each. Assemble the blocks with finishing strips (see page 22). Assemble the rows with finishing strips.

Finishing the Quilt

The quilt interior should measure 60½" by 80½" (153.7 by 204.5 cm). Cut borders as shown below.

BORDER MEASUREMENTS—Cut 2 each		
3" Finished 1st border	sides	3½" x 80½"
	top, bottom	3½" x 66½"
2" Finished 2nd border	sides	2½" x 86½"
	top, bottom	2½" x 70½"
5" Finished 3rd border	sides	5½" x 90½"
	top, bottom	5½" x 80½"

Use the six-layer seam method illustrated with World Without End on pages 9 and 10 for adding 3" first border. Add the 2" and 5" borders using the stitch and flip method on page 10. Finish the quilt with a ½" French-fold binding.

Use the six-layer seam method illustrated with World Without End on pages 9 and 10 for adding 3" first border. Add the 2" and 5" borders using the stitch and flip method on page 10.

World Without End—King-size Version

To make a king-size version of World Without End, make 64 blocks and combine to make 16 quilting units. Join the quilted units into four horizontal rows of four units each. The completed quilt interior should measure 80½" square.

Finish the quilt with 4", 3" and 5" borders, and a ½" French-fold binding. The quilt will be approximately 104" (264.2 cm) square.

Perfect Patchwork Templates Set Q, Product #8212 and Set T, Product #8203, are available from Michell Marketing, Inc., or ask for them at your favorite quilt shop.

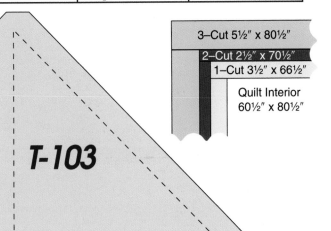

3—Cut 5½" x 80½"
2—Cut 2½" x 70½"
1—Cut 3½" x 66½"
Quilt Interior
60½" x 80½"

T-103

Cut 5⅞" squares in half diagonally. Use corners of Template #94 to blunt these corners.

A

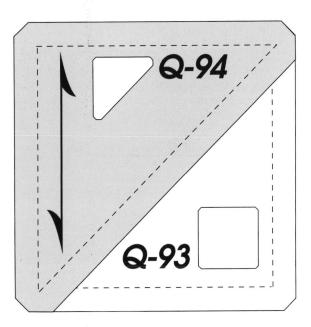

Q-94

Q-93

Full Size Patterns for World Without End

Numbers correspond to the silkscreened numbers on templates in **From MARTI MICHELL** Perfect Patchwork Template Set Q or Set T.

Not Such Hard Times

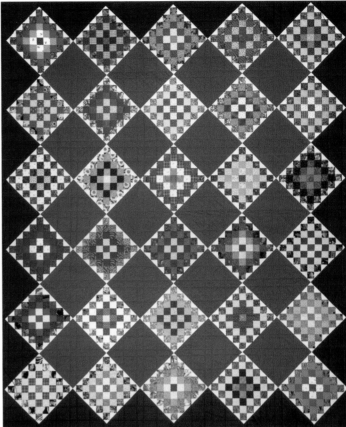

Approximate Finished Size: 87¾″ x 105″ (223 cm x 267 cm)

In the photograph shown above, the antique quilt hanging on the door is called Tennessee Hard Times. It was the inspiration for Not Such Hard Times, shown here and on the cover. You can see that the antique quilt was a product of an era whose theme was "Use it up, wear it out, make do, or do without." Some of the blocks use random fabric and color placement; others are much more consistent and organized. The Not Such Hard Times scrap quilt interprets the design in a more orderly fashion. The fabric used in each position is consistent in each patchwork block, but each block uses a different combination of fabrics.

This quilt is in my book *Quilting for People Who STILL Don't Have Time to Quilt*. However, in that book we ran out of space to describe how it was actually quilted by the section. This is a classic diagonal set quilt. That means that when it is pieced, the rows run diagonally across the quilt. So that is how it was divided for quilting. Any diagonal set quilt with seams that go edge to edge can be divided in the same manner. (See Vintage Dresden Plate, page 38, for an example of a diagonal set quilt that does not have edge-to-edge seams.)

Look at the photo of this quilt in sections, page 53. There are three diagonal strips that are two blocks wide. Think how much easier it is to quilt a long 24″ wide strip than a full-size quilt. There are two corner sections that are somewhat triangular. They could have been divided, but it didn't seem necessary. In the picture, the sections are layered on batting and backing and have actually been quilted.

Issues	Answers
1. This will be a very large diagonal set patchwork quilt with no borders.	**1.** Easily divided into diagonal rows the full width of the quilt.
2. "In the ditch" quilting will go to the edge of block.	**2.** Join units with finishing strips.

Now look at the back of the quilt, pictured below. Three fabrics were selected to make the back more interesting. Because the quilting went all the way to the edge of the strips, it was necessary to join the sections with finishing strips (see page 22). The finishing strips were cut to match one of the two fabrics at a seam; it didn't really matter which fabric was used. In the detail photo of the quilt back you can barely see a finishing strip.

FINISHED SIZES
Quilt Size: 87¾" by 105" (222.9 cm by 266.7 cm)
Block Size: 12¼" (31.1 cm) square

MATERIALS REQUIRED
1½ yards total of three assorted fabrics for position #1 (monochromatic ecru print)
2⅛ yards total of assorted fabrics for position #2 (large print)*
1⅝ yards total of assorted fabrics for position #3*
1⅛ yards total of assorted fabrics for position #4*
⅞ yard total of assorted fabrics for position #5*
¾ yard total of assorted fabrics for position #6*
3 yards of fabric for alternate blocks
2 yards of contrasting fabric for setting and corner triangles
7⅞ yards total of fabric for backing fabric and finishing strips
King size batting or equivalent
⅞ yard of fabric for French-fold binding
*assorted fat quarters may be used to equal the total fabric requirement

Selecting the Fabric
While every fabric in every block doesn't have to be different, fabric collectors like me love to select just the right 150 fabrics for this quilt. If you really want to be popular, cut additional sets of strips when you cut— they are a perfect gift for a quilting friend!

The non-pieced alternating block is a dark red print fabric. It was selected first, then six different non-directional fabrics were selected for each block. The fabric used in position #1 (the setting and corner triangles of the block) is always an ecru on ecru in this quilt. Fabric position #2 is what could be called the theme print for the block. In this quilt it is usually multicolored and a relatively large print. Fabrics were not considered for theme if they were ugly with the alternate block fabric, but they might clash slightly. It is easy to make a boring quilt if you pick only fabrics that are very pretty with the alternating block fabric.

The fabrics in the other block positions coordinate with the theme fabric, but without a specific order of color value. Some blocks shade light to dark, some alternate light and dark prints, some have high contrast, and some have almost no contrast.

Cutting the Fabric for the Scrap Patchwork Block
Traditional quilt books would instruct you to cut 41 squares, 16 setting triangles and 4 corner triangles or 61 separate pieces for each block, and to assemble them individually. But why would you do that, when Sew-Before-You-Cut strip techniques allow you to make the blocks more accurately, and in a fraction of the time? Sometimes people who are making scrap quilts overlook the ease of incorporating strip techniques. Hopefully, the method for making this scrappy quilt block will remind you to try strip techniques.

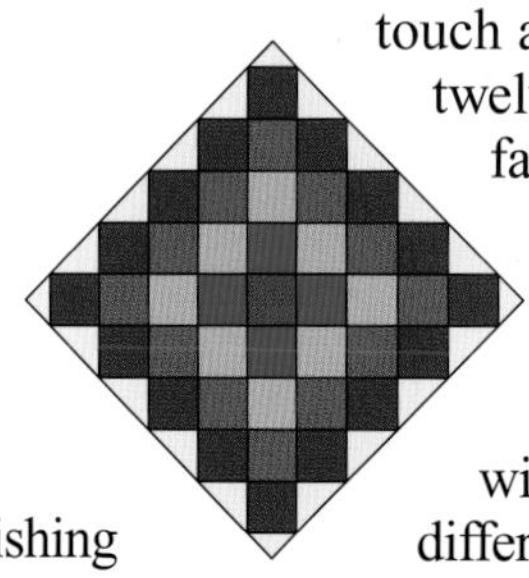

Examine the block and you will see the fabrics repeating in the same order from the outside in. Fabrics 1 and 2 always touch and if you look again, fabric #3 is next to #2 twelve times. Likewise, all eight squares of the #4 fabric always touch a #3. It seems like a good idea to sew strips of each fabric together instead of individual squares. However, if the strips are all cut the same length and sewn into sets, there will be too many squares and "reverse sewing" will be necessary. That is why we have calculated the different lengths necessary for each fabric based on the number of squares required.

| STRIP | TOTAL LENGTH NEEDED | CUTTING IN SECTIONS | |
| | | SECTION A | SECTION B |
		Illustrated on page 51	
#1 Bias Strip	2½" x 32"	2½" x 18"	2½" x 18"
#2 Strip	2¼" x 36"	2¼" x 18"	2¼" x 18"
#3 Strip	2¼" x 27"	2¼" x 18"	2¼" x 9"
#4 Strip	2¼" x 18"	2¼" x 18"	
#5 Strip	2¼" x 9"	2¼" x 9"	

(OR)

1. Refer to the cutting chart to determine the length of cut strips for each fabric in each patchwork block. Cut all strips except #1 on the lengthwise grain. I prefer strips cut on the lengthwise grain because they will remain straight, with virtually no arcing or bowing, when sewn together. If you are working with fat quarters, the 18″ lengthwise strip can be cut exactly into eight 2¼″ strip sets, with no room for error.

2. Cut one 2¼″ square from fabric #6, the center square.

3. Because the squares in each block are set diagonally, small corner triangles are needed for each block. For each block, cut two 3″ squares from fabric #1. Cut squares in half diagonally to yield four corner triangles. For the fabric #1 setting triangles, see the Bias Strip Trick below.

A Bias Strip Trick: Bias Strip Replaces Setting Triangles

Since this block is like a small quilt set on point, and each block has 20 setting triangles, there are 600 tiny setting triangles in this quilt. Even using quick cutting methods or templates, that sounds like a lot of triangles; there must be an easier way! There is; and it's a wonderful trick, especially useful for small setting triangles like these. Use the instructions that follow to replace the setting triangles with a bias strip. When the block is complete, there will be excess fabric on the outer edges of the block. Cut it off to make a square, and you will have created perfect setting triangles with straight grain on the outer edge.

How to Cut Bias

In order to allow for seam allowances after trimming the blocks, the bias strips are cut ¼″ wider than the other strips.

Cut bias from half-yard pieces of at least three different ecru print fabrics. The easiest way is to first square off one end of the fabric. Align a 45-degree angle or ruler with one straight edge of the fabric and cut away a small triangle. Then cut 2½″ wide strips following the 45-degree angle.

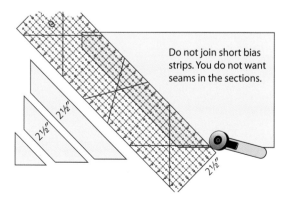

Do not join short bias strips. You do not want seams in the sections.

Assembling the Patchwork Block

All the fabrics in each numbered position are consistent within each block, but each block uses a different combination of fabrics.

1. Cut two squares from the bias #1 fabric. They are the two single squares in the layouts.

2. Join fabric strips #2, #3, #4 and #5 into strip sets as shown, whether one or two sections. Press all seam allowances in the same direction. Cut across in 2¼″ increments to make two sets of squares.

3. Add bias strip #1 to the remaining strip set, as shown, and continue cutting 14 more 2¼″ strip sets.

4.

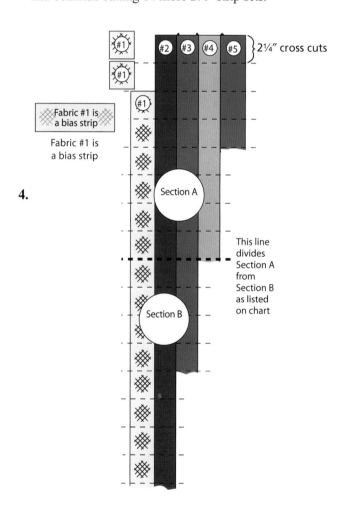

2¼″ cross cuts

Fabric #1 is a bias strip

Fabric #1 is a bias strip

Section A

Section B

This line divides Section A from Section B as listed on chart

---

You should have the number of sets of squares shown:

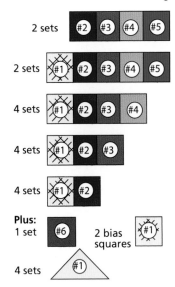

2 sets   #2 #3 #4 #5

2 sets   #1 #2 #3 #4 #5

4 sets   #1 #2 #3 #4

4 sets   #1 #2 #3

4 sets   #1 #2

Plus:
1 set   #6   2 bias squares   #1

4 sets   #1

5. Lay out the rows for each block as shown. Don't forget, half of the units will be rotated 180 degrees to make the block.

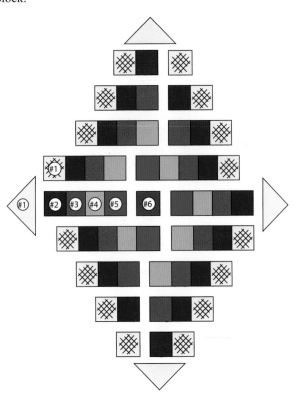

6. Join the sets of squares and single squares into rows. Press all seams in one direction. Join the rows. Reverse the rows to get opposing seam allowances. Add corner triangles to complete 30 blocks.

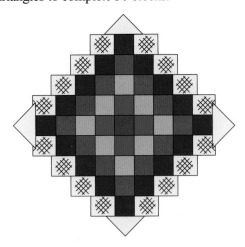

7. Use an acrylic ruler and rotary cutter to trim the blocks. Line up the ruler on the block so that the ¼″ mark consistently passes through the block at the point where you want a seam. When the excess is cut away, a ¼″ seam allowance will be left.

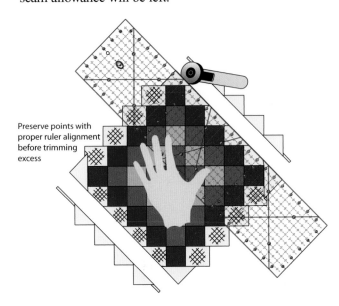

Preserve points with proper ruler alignment before trimming excess

The block should measure 12¾″ square, including seam allowances.

Adding the Alternate Blocks

If your patchwork blocks are not 12¾″ square, substitute their measurement for the steps in this section.

1. Cut 10 strips of background fabric, 12¾″ wide by 27″ long.

2. Chain piece 20 of the patchwork blocks to the strips of background fabric. Press seam allowances toward the background fabric.

3. Using the patchwork blocks and a ruler as guides, cut across the strips in 12¾" increments, creating 20 pairs of blocks.

Joining the Rows

Using a slightly darker red fabric for the setting and corner triangles created the subtle border look.

1. To make setting triangles, use the **From Marti Michell** large Diagonal Set Triangle Ruler or cut five 19½" squares from background fabric. Cut each square on both diagonals to yield 20 setting triangles; 18 are required.

2. For the corner triangles, use the **From Marti Michell** large Diagonal Set Triangle Ruler or cut two 12¼" squares. Cut each square once diagonally to yield four corner triangles.

3. Lay out the blocks in diagonal rows, as shown. Add setting and corner triangles and the remaining 10 patchwork blocks.

4. Continue assembling the quilt as shown for the five sections. Identification notes will help keep the blocks in the desired positions.

Finishing the Quilt

Layer as shown. Quilt in sections. Join with finishing strips. Trim edges and square up corners. Bind, see pages 69 and 70.

The **From Marti Michell** *large Diagonal Set Triangle Ruler, Product #8968, is available from Michell Marketing, Inc., or ask for it at your favorite quilt shop. Also available: The large No-Flip Diagonal Set Triangle Ruler, Product #8104.*

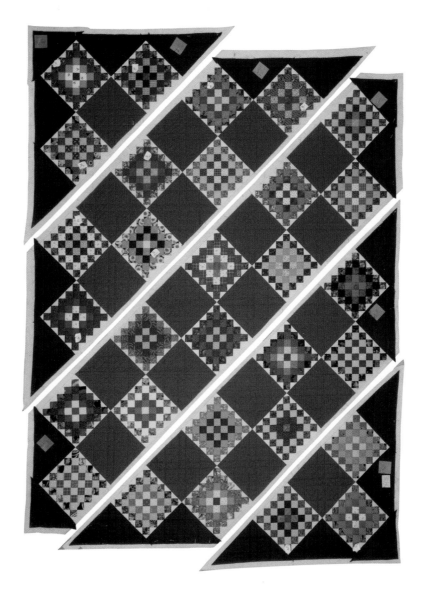

Primrose Lane

Approximate Finished Size: 81½″ x 97½″ (207 cm x 247.7 cm)

The original blue and rose Primrose Lane quilt above was made for a "Not So Block of the Month" program with Maywood Studio. To test the instructions, I started a second quilt in black and brown. The operative word is "started."

Now I realize, left in sections, it is a great teaching sample! The colors used in these instructions are inspired by the black and brown Primrose Lane that follows.

Issues	Answers
1. Primrose Lane is a big quilt, 81½″ x 97½″.	**1.** Plan to quilt in sections.
2. Cotton batting planned for the black and brown Primrose Lane can "bulk up" when sewn into seams.	**2.** Cut cotton batting to the finished size of sections so it will not be sewn into seams.
3. The zigzag border does not permit the straight seam needed in a few places to make easy-to-assemble units.	**3.** Easy! Cut 8 #9 triangles to be used in place of four 9+9 triangles.

All of the pattern pieces and minimal piecing instructions are included for Primrose Lane. The numbers on the patterns and the illustrations match the acrylic pieces in **From Marti Michell** Perfect Patchwork Template Sets B and D.

MATERIALS REQUIRED

3½ yards black for last border and blocks
2½ yards stripe for sawtooth border and medallion border
1¾ yards red for border and Piece of Cake blocks
1⅛ yard turquoise (⅜ yard each of three)
1 yard black for baskets in border
1 yard cream for background in large blocks
½ yard for background for Old Maid's Walk blocks
½ yard red for Old Maid's Walk blocks
½ yard background for medallion center
½ yard for background of second border on medallion center
⅞ yard for binding
Batting to accommodate sections of quilt
6½ yards backing fabric
Feel free to combine yardage requirements and use fewer fabrics, or add more fabric for variety.

Cutting

Each block has both a color key and a pattern key. The colors in the blocks represent suggested fabric placements. When you have decided on your fabric selections, multiply the number of pieces in a block by the number of blocks and cut the required fabrics for your quilt.

Making the Patchwork Units

1. Make five Square Within a Square blocks.

Add #13 triangles to opposite sides of the #10 square. Press seam allowances toward the triangles. Then add the remaining #13 triangles. Continue in the same way with the #11 and #9 triangles. The blocks should measure 8½", including seam allowances.

2. Make eight Old Maid's Walk blocks.

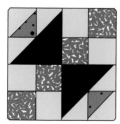
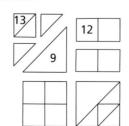

Make 16 four-patch units and 16 of the pieced triangle units, and combine as shown. The blocks should be 8½", including seam allowances.

3. The complicated look of the center medallion is deceiving; it is really very simple construction. However, it is perfect for cutting and arranging on a design wall until you really like the results. Retrieve one of the Square Within a Square blocks for the very center. For ease of construction, pay careful attention to the numbers shown on the layout and to the sub-units shown.

Number 23 is asymmetrical. Cut those pieces with the fabric right sides together to cut #23 and #23(r–reverse) at the same time.

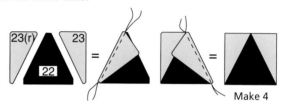

When you like the selected fabrics, complete the sewing. The center unit should be 24½" square, including seam allowances.

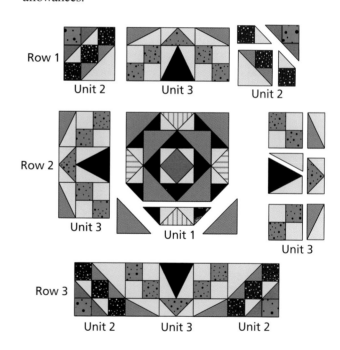

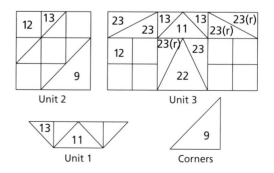

When two thin #23 triangles are sewn together to make a rectangle, they align at several match points in a slightly different way than most corners.

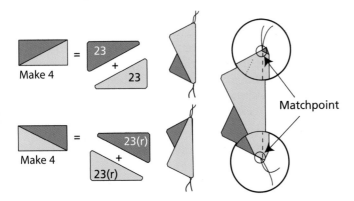

Matchpoint

4. Use Triangle #22 to trim one end of a 4½″ wide strip. Measure 12½″ and position #22 as shown below to trim the other corners and cut the 4 center trapezoids in the first border of the medallion.

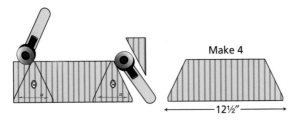

Make 4

——— 12½″ ———

5. Make two and add to sides of center medallion:

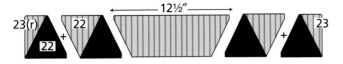

——— 12½″ ———

23(r)   22   22   23

6. Make two:

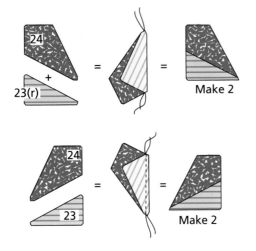

24
23(r)   =   =   Make 2

24
23   =   =   Make 2

7. Assemble the final border sections and add to the top and bottom of the center medallion.

8. Cut 36 #10 squares, 68 #11 triangles and eight #13 triangles for the second border of the medallion center. To reduce stretching, cut the #11 triangles with the long side on straight grain. Assemble into four corner units and four border units, as shown. Add borders in the numerical order shown, taking advantage of a partial seam at the right end of the first border attached. Add the corner units. The center section should now be 40½″ square, including seam allowances. It is ready to be layered and quilted.

1. Leave end unstitched

5. Complete partial seam

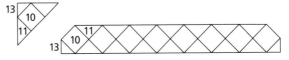

13   10
11

11
13   10

9. This next group is affectionately called the Hodge Podge blocks. They aren't recognized patchwork blocks, just units that will create a pleasing background for the more dramatic blocks. Make as shown.

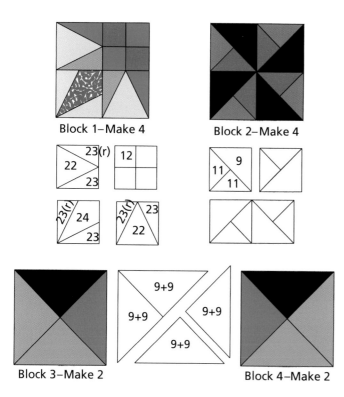

Block 1–Make 4   Block 2–Make 4

Block 3–Make 2   Block 4–Make 2

10. Making the Piece of Cake blocks will probably take the most time, but they add dramatic detail around the edge of the bed. Make sure you have selected high contrast fabrics for the small triangles that create the Bear's Paw or Cake Stand-type units.

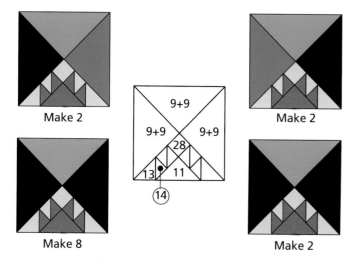

Make 2   Make 2

Make 8   Make 2

Remember, you are not going to join all of the pieces. You are joining the pieces into the sections shown on page 58.

Making the Border Units

The blue and rose Primrose Lane was quilted in one piece. The black and brown Primrose Lane had to have minor alterations to create convenient sections. Four large 9+9 triangles in the border needed to be divided and cut as eight #9 triangles.

The quantities and measurements for the strips and squares for the borders are on the quilt diagram on page 58. Cut the following number of triangles:

64	9+9 Triangles and 16 #9 Triangles from the stripe fabric for the Sawtooth border.
14	9+9 Triangles from the black basket fabric
4	9+9 Triangles from the turquoise fabric
52	9+9 Triangles from the last border fabric

Take time to "nub off" the corners, as shown on the pattern, and the pieces will fit perfectly for piecing.

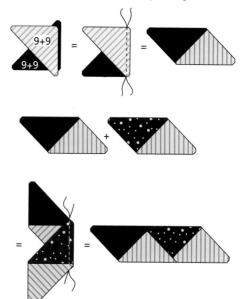

The quilt borders on the top and left of this diagram show the sizes of strips and squares to cut, or the numbers of the pattern pieces to use. They also show the general assembly order.

The same sections on the right side and bottom show the fabrics used and are stitched.

How the sections are joined will depend on how you quilt and your personal preference. Review Chapter 3, starting on page 16.

The black and brown Primrose Lane quilt has cotton batting. For some time, I have warned students that cotton batting is much more dense than polyester, and makes a heavier seam when quilted in sections and assembled with finishing strips. Because it was clear that the quilting would go to the edge of most of the separate sections, the cotton batting was cut the finished size, no seam allowances included, before layering. This made it necessary to be more careful when layering. Even though the quilt is not completely assembled, enough has been completed to know the seams will be very acceptable.

Because the front of this quilt has a lot of activity, the back was planned using three fabrics to create a simple reversible pattern. The center section was quilted first. The size of the center made it a nice manageable square. I did machine-guided modified outline quilting, and machine-guided quilting in the ditch, as well as considerable free-motion quilting.

In the photograph below, the end piece at the right is layered, quilted and trimmed, ready for final sewing. The same section on the left has the final Flying Geese border pinned in place, ready to stitch and flip.

The center side section at the top is layered and quilted but not trimmed. The center side section at the bottom and the center medallion are quilted and trimmed. The final borders for the long edges of the quilt are hanging on the small frame and will be added with batting and backing using a six-layer seam when the quilt is assembled more fully.

Primrose Lane *was a design developed for a Maywood Studio "Not So Block of the Month" program.*

Full Size Patterns for Primrose Lane

Numbers correspond to the silkscreened numbers on templates in **From Marti Michell** Perfect Patchwork Template Sets B and D.

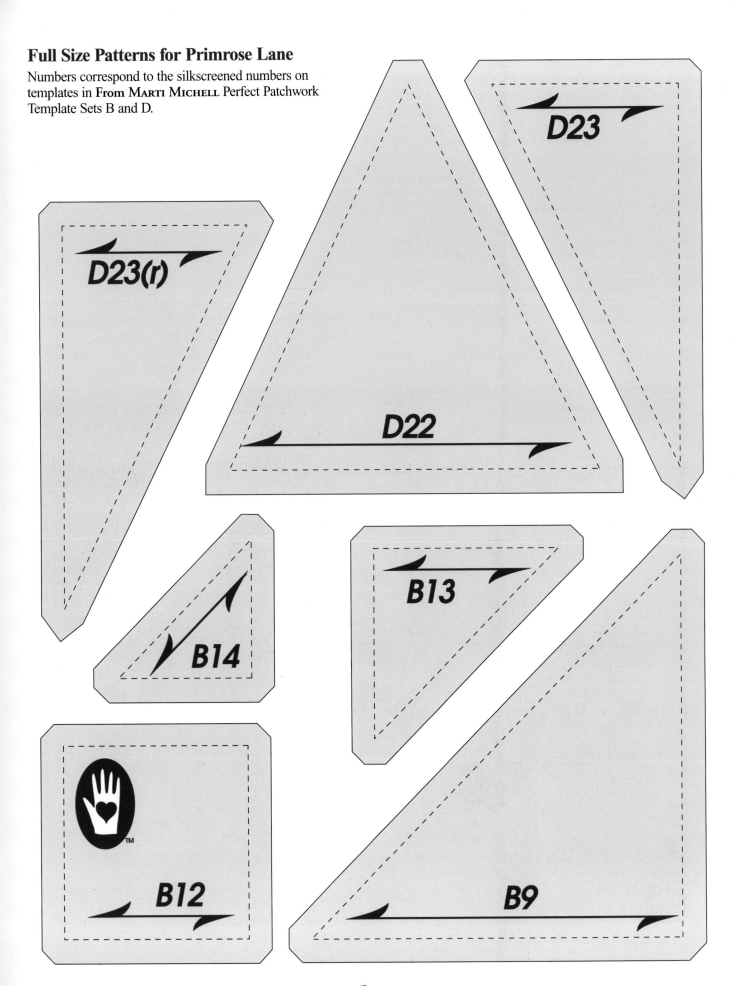

Full Size Patterns for Primrose Lane

Numbers correspond to the silkscreened numbers on templates in **FROM MARTI MICHELL** Perfect Patchwork Template Sets B and D.

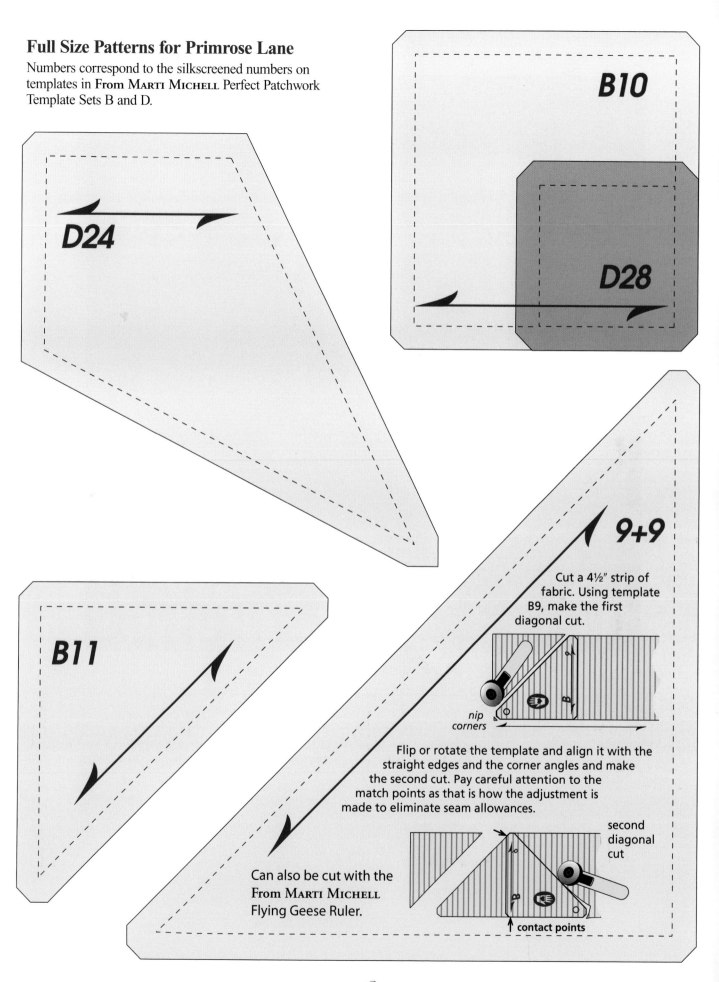

B10

D24

D28

9+9

Cut a 4½" strip of fabric. Using template B9, make the first diagonal cut.

nip corners

Flip or rotate the template and align it with the straight edges and the corner angles and make the second cut. Pay careful attention to the match points as that is how the adjustment is made to eliminate seam allowances.

B11

second diagonal cut

Can also be cut with the **FROM MARTI MICHELL** Flying Geese Ruler.

contact points

Picnic Basket Quilt

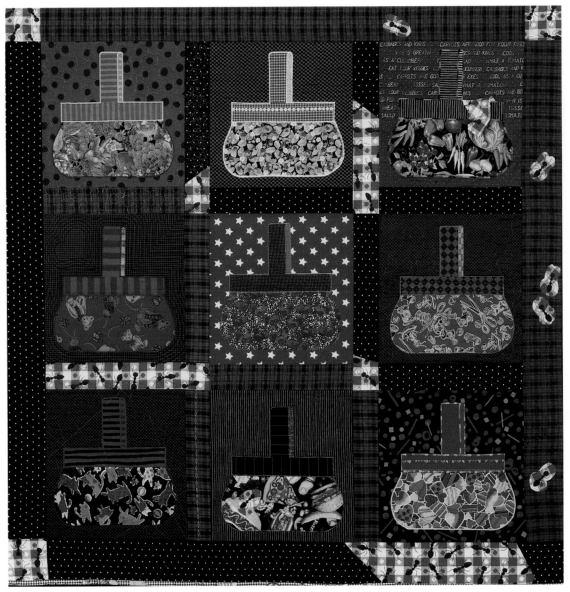

Approximate Finished Size: 54¾″ (139.1 cm) square

Issues	Answers
1. Quilting will include dense machine guided built-in programmed stitches and each block will be quilted differently.	**1.** Divide into sections. In this case, blocks and sashing strips are combined for greater maneuverability.
2. Quilting would go to the edge of many blocks.	**2.** Join with aligned finishing strips (see page 64).
3. Section sizes accommodate using the stitch and flip technique for the sashing. What about the border?	**3.** Add the border using the six-layer seam method, page 20.
4. Planned to use cotton batting.	**4.** To reduce bulk in the finishing strips and six-layer seam on border, trim batting out of seam allowances. Quilting will secure batting enough.
5. The blocks are directional.	**5.** Be careful when joining!

FINISHED SIZES
Quilt Size: 54¾″ (139.1 cm)
Block Size: 14″ (35.6 cm) square

MATERIALS REQUIRED
Nine assorted 16″ squares for block backgrounds
Nine assorted 6″ by 13″ scraps for appliquéd baskets
Nine assorted 5″ by 11″ scraps for appliquéd rims
  and handles
2⅛ yards of paper-backed fusible product
½ yard of fabric for sashing (assorted scraps, if desired)
4⅛ yards of fabric for backing, including finishing strips,
  or nine assorted pieces, minimum 18″ square
⅞ yard of fabric for border (assorted scraps, if desired)
3½ yards of cotton batting, or twin size packaged batting
⅝ yard of fabric for French-fold binding

About the Quilt

This quilt is all about selecting fun fabrics and embellishing them with interesting sewing machine stitches. Because every basket and every background fabric is different, it's fun to quilt every block differently.

Selecting the Fabric

Twenty-seven different prints are showcased in this wall hanging. The fabrics chosen for the baskets themselves reflect the many things that might be found in my picnic baskets. Contrasting handles and bands, and geometric print backgrounds complete the quilt blocks. Sashing strips and borders were pieced from several prints, most notably a fabric designed as a red and white checked tablecloth, complete with ants. This fabric continues the theme, and says it all for me about picnics! I used the fusible appliqué technique to randomly place ants from this fabric on the quilt border, also.

Cutting the Fabric

Typically, quilt blocks are the same size. However, in this quilt, I wanted to incorporate sashing strips into the Quilt-As-You-Sew blocks. That resulted in four different block sizes, as you can see in the quilt assembly layout on page 64.

An 18″ square for the block with two sashing strips was the largest backing piece needed. It is easier to cut all backing and batting pieces 18″ square and trim away any extra as you work, than to keep track of cutting four different sizes of backing and batting for different combinations of blocks and sashing strips.

1. Cut nine 14½″ squares from assorted fabrics for the basket backgrounds. Cut nine 18″ squares of backing fabric and batting.

2. Press paper-backed fusible product to the wrong side of the nine basket fabrics. Using the patterns on page 65, cut nine Picnic Baskets. Cut nine matching Basket Handles and Basket Rims to coordinate with the baskets. To create the illusion of dimension, a small piece of fabric representing the inside of the basket handle is fused beside the handle. In all the baskets shown, this fabric is just the wrong side of the handle fabric. Press paper-backed fusible product to the right side of these scraps for Inside Basket Handles. Cut nine.

3. Cut 12 sashing strips from assorted fabric, 3″ wide by 14½″ long. Cut four 3″ squares of assorted fabric for corner blocks. The quilt shown has pieced fabric strips in some sashing strips.

Fusing the Baskets

Fuse all baskets, handles and rims in place. A small scrap of fabric was arranged as a napkin and tucked "inside" (underneath) one basket before fusing the basket into place. Because this is a Quilt-As-You-Sew project, do not sew around the edges of the baskets until the quilt block is layered with batting and backing.

Preparing the Blocks for Assembly

1. Lay a backing square wrong side up, with a batting square on top.

2. Layer a fused block on top of the batting, carefully matching all raw edges at top left corner of block. Repeat for all squares.

3. Arrange the blocks in three rows of three blocks each, according to your preferred layout. Label each block according to its position, such as Row 1, Block A. We have abbreviated block positions to 1A, et cetera.

Adding the Sashing

1. Study the assembly diagram on page 64 carefully. Sew a 3″ square to one end of four bottom sashing strips.

2. Sashing strips are added using the stitch and flip method (see page 10). Sew a sashing strip to the right side of blocks 1A, 1B, 2A, 2B, 3A, and 3B. Sew a sashing strip to the bottom of blocks 1C and 2C. Sew a sashing strips with corner square to the bottom of blocks 1A, 1B, 2A, and 2B.

Quilting the Blocks

Because the baskets are fused in place, the edges can be secured with machine zigzag stitching now. This is a good place to experiment with decorative machine stitches and specialty threads such as metallic and variegated colors. Do not quilt into the seam allowance, so you will be able to trim batting away before joining the blocks. Separate blocks made it easy to maneuver the blocks during quilting. If I had not been doing such elaborate quilting and decorative stitching on these blocks, they could have been assembled into three rows for quilting.

Trimming the Blocks

1. Trim the blocks to size carefully, allowing for seam allowances on all sides. This is most easily done with a large acrylic square and a rotary cutter.

   • Trim Blocks 1A, 1B, 2A, and 2B to 17" square.

   • Trim Blocks 1C and 2C to 14½" wide by 17" long.

   • Trim Blocks 3A and 3B to 17" wide by 14½" long.

   • Trim Block 3C to 14½" square.

2. Assuming you have quilted the sashing securely, use scissors to trim the batting an additional ¼", so it will not be caught in the seam allowance when joining blocks into rows, or when adding the border.

Assembling the Blocks into Rows

1. Assemble the blocks into three horizontal rows of three blocks each.

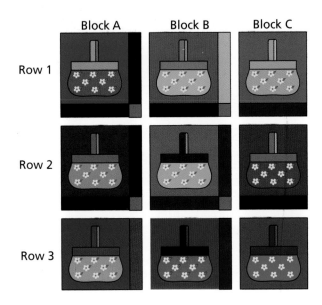

| | Block A | Block B | Block C |

2. Because the seams used to add the sashing strips extend to the edge of the block, separate finishing strips must be used to join the blocks into rows. (See page 22.) Cut four finishing strips on the lengthwise grain, 1½" wide by 18½" long, and two strips 1½" wide by 16" long for Row 3. Press the strips in half lengthwise with wrong sides together. See Alternating or Aligned Finishing Strips, below, to decide on which block to place the strip.

Alternating or Aligned Finishing Strips

The finishing strip extends from the seam line approximately ½" onto the back of the block it was not touching when the seam was sewn. If you want the strips to alternate from row to row—which reduces bulk at the intersection of four blocks—then practice alternate positioning. On Row 1, all of the strips are placed on the block that will be to the left. On Row 2 they are on the block that will be to the right. On Row 3, they will be back to the left, etc.

Alternating finishing strips

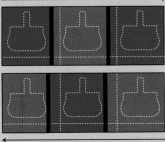

Sometimes it is fun to line up the strips and make a continuous grid in a contrasting fabric on the back of the quilt. In that case, all strips should be placed consistently on the block that will be to the right all the way through. Or, strips can be consistently placed on the block that will be to the left.

Aligned finishing strips

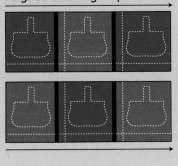

Joining the Rows

Finishing strips are used to join the three rows of blocks to each other. Cut two strips of fabric 1½" wide by 49" long. When the quilt interior is completed, it should measure 47½" square, including seam allowances.

Adding the Borders and Binding

1. The border for the quilt shown was pieced from assorted scraps in the same manner as sashing strips. Whether pieced or unpieced, two borders should be 4″ wide by 47½″ long, and two should be 4″ by 54½″. Cut two strips each of batting and border backing fabric 5½″ by 47½″, and two strips 5½″ by 57″.

2. Add the sides, then the top and bottom, using the six-layer seam method, page 20.

3. A separate ⅜″ French-fold binding is used to finish the quilt. See page 69 for details.

Full Size Patterns for Picnic Basket Quilt

All pieces are fused. No seam allowances are included in the patterns.

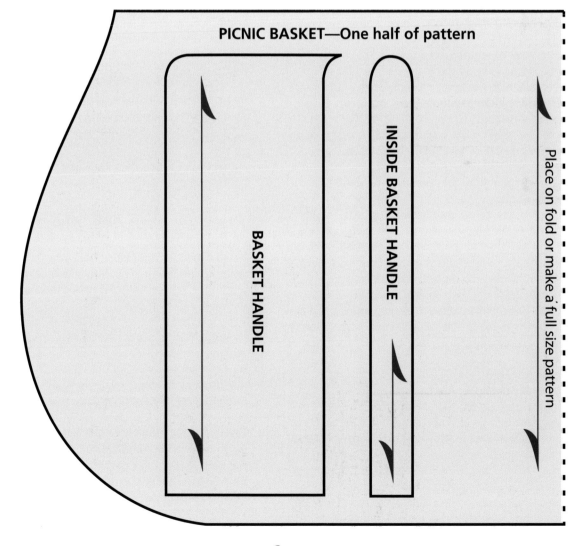

BASKET RIM—One half of pattern

PICNIC BASKET—One half of pattern

BASKET HANDLE

INSIDE BASKET HANDLE

Place on fold or make a full size pattern

Chapter 6

Marti's Rules
for Machine Quilting

As I said earlier, this is not a basic machine quilting book. There are many of those, including my own *Learn to Machine Quilt in Just One Weekend*. This is simply a short list of machine quilting tips—but, in case this is your first book on machine quilting, we review basic information about layering and quilting in sections (see page 67). Machine quilting is a skill where the methods need to fit you and your machine. If my methods don't feel right for you, please try someone else's style or experiment on your own. However, there are a few things that are nearly imperative, no matter how you machine quilt.

Bond with your machine. You might say that machine quilting is a team sport. If you love your machine and already let it do hems and tucks and decorative stitching for you, machine quilting will probably be a snap. If you don't like your machine you probably won't like machine quilting. If you "can't stand your machine," trying to learn to quilt with it may send you to the funny farm.

Be fair to your machine. It is possible you don't like your machine because you don't know how to use it well enough. Before you reject your machine, give it a good chance. To be really fair, you may need to spend a weekend together and really get in touch with your machine. Time spent preparing your machine to quilt allows you to deepen the relationship between you and your machine.

If you can't bond with the machine you have, get a new one. If you have decided that you and your current machine have irreconcilable differences, shop carefully for a new machine.

Get your space in shape. Just because quilting is at the bottom of the exercise list, that doesn't mean we can't get our sewing area into good shape. A table that the machine fits into, or a lowered table with an acrylic surround, large flat surfaces to help hold the quilt, tall tables to pin on, a good adjustable-height rolling chair, and good lighting are all very crucial to your success at machine quilting. If what you try first is not comfortable, please don't give up machine quilting without trying some different solutions.

The right tools make the job easy. Make sure your needle and thread are compatible. Generally, use as small a needle as the thread will allow. Don't wait to change the needle on your machine until it is broken; a fresh needle for each project is a good rule.

Start small. The first step in starting small is referring to physical size: pillows, vests while they are flat, and crib quilts are all good for your first efforts at machine quilting. However, start small emotionally, too. Printed quilt panels are fun because you have no personal investment in them. That is, you won't "ruin" something you have already spent many hours in making. As a bonus, the quilted item can be used for a gift.

Think seriously about ways to work in sections on any project. Most quilt books and patterns aren't written for working in sections, but this one is!

Expect to practice. You know the old joke. "How do you get to Carnegie Hall?"

Practice, practice, practice.

Don't expect to be satisfied with your first effort at machine quilting. Just like it is necessary to practice machine quilting, it is necessary to practice machine quilting in sections.

Breathe. It is amazing how many people who are machine quilting actually discover they are holding their breath. If music helps you relax, quilt to music. Many people feel that listening to music while they quilt helps them breathe, as well as creates a good rhythm in their work.

Enjoy. Taking frequent breaks helps to change any stress on the muscles. When you are concentrating on the stitching, it is easy to lose track of your position or how long you have been in it. Quilting in sections has a bonus—when you finish a section, you have to move!

Layering and Quilting in Sections

Layering and quilting in sections is a simplified version of doing the same thing for a full-size bed quilt. It is most like layering and quilting a crib quilt or wall hanging and is really quite simple. As the quilts get larger, there are more variations, questions and difficulties that may arise, which is why we are quilting in sections.

1. The backing fabric should be 2″ to 4″ bigger in all directions than the size of the finished section. You should not have to piece the backing in most quilt sections, but you may choose to (see the back photo of Bed of Roses, page 28). Cut the batting the same size as the backing, steaming to remove wrinkles and bumps, if necessary. (See Preparing the Batting, pages 17 and 18.)

2. Use a table, with a surface you can't hurt, for the layering process. Center the backing wrong side up on the table. Tape or clamp the backing fabric in place, so that it is taut, with no wrinkles, but not stretched. A stretched backing fabric will relax and become smaller when removed from the table. So, don't stretch it, unless you are trying to create the washed and shrunken antique look. Layer the batting next, centered and carefully smoothed. Finally, center and layer the pressed quilt top, right side up.

3. Baste. I have used small (size #1) rustproof nickel safety pins for years and prefer them to thread basting. Some people are very fond of the basting guns, but since I have a lifetime supply of safety pins, I have not switched. Start in the center and work out, pinning through all layers. The minimum number of pins on a typical 40″ by 60″ crib quilt is one every few inches in both directions, or just over 100 pins. It is better to start with more pins than you think you need and reduce the number as you become more experienced.

Spray adhesives and fusible batting have also become readily available in the last few years. While I still love my safety pins and Kwik Klip™ pin closer, I have tried both the spray adhesive and fusible batting. They both seem much more appropriate for quilting in sections than for full size bed quilts. Instead of layering on a table when using the spray adhesive, I worked vertically at the design wall, and in sections, from the top down.

Machine and Body Position

Before you do much quilting, let's get serious about the space in which you work. Being ergonomically correct is especially important when you start machine quilting because you generally sit for a longer period of time than for other sewing. Most of your other sewing steps are broken up with changing position to press, cut, et cetera. Machine quilting is also more intense for most people, which means you need the best physical setting possible.

For me, it is imperative that my work area be level with the bed of my machine. That means my machine is either set into a table so that the bed of the machine is level with the tabletop or on a lower table, such as some computer tables, with a portable surround. If you put the machine and portable surround on top of your standard table, you have a nicely enlarged working surface, which is good. The bad news is that most tables are around 30″ high, making your work surface around 33″ to 34″ high—too high. However, if you place the machine and acrylic platform on a computer table that is usually around 27″ high—or better yet, adjustable—the surface of the machine will be at a comfortable level. The acrylic platform shown in the photograph on page 29 is the Sew Steady Portable Table from Sew Steady.

Regardless of the height of your machine, your body needs to be high enough that your forearms can rest comfortably on the edge of the table. The best solution is an adjustable height office chair. I have also used a mid-height stool to raise the height of my torso but still allows me to have my feet on the floor and a resting spot for my seat. The point is to avoid having to hold your arms up during this process, and to put your eyes in a position to see where you are stitching.

Under the Table

Most machines have a foot-operated speed control pedal, and it is not unusual to have it scoot around. The scooting foot pedal is one of those things that you tend to follow subconsciously, contorting your body, stretching your leg and back muscles in unnecessary and unhealthy ways. Most of the sewing machine stores or mail-order sewing catalogs sell a little rubber mat that will keep the foot pedal stationary. Treat yourself to one and save your back. A home remedy if you have a carpeted sewing area is to put the hook half of an adhesive-backed Velcro® strip on the bottom of the foot control. It will catch in the carpet and prevent the pedal from moving.

Quilting In the Ditch

1. If you have an even-feed attachment, now is the time to attach it, or if your machine has built-in even feed, make sure it is engaged. Remember, the quilt is multi-layered and only the bottom layer comes in contact with the feed dogs that pull the fabric during the machine guided

sewing. The even-feed attachments are designed to pull the top layer at the same rate as the bottom and prevent wrinkling.

2. Putting a fresh needle in the machine when you start a new project is a good idea. For most in-the-ditch quilting, I like to use the smoky invisible monofilament thread for the top thread only. In the bobbin, I use a good quality 100% cotton or cotton-wrapped polyester thread that matches the color of the backing fabric. It is usually necessary to loosen the tension when using the monofilament thread. It is very stretchy and if the tension is too tight, the thread stretches while being sewn so it draws up and puckers when you stop sewing. Use a stitch length of 8 to 10 stitches per inch (2.5 to 3.0 on metric machines) for quilting.

3. To keep a large quilt section manageable when machine quilting, it is necessary to roll and fold it into a smaller package. The longest center seam is the first seam that will be sewn. I like to roll the right edge of the quilt and fold the left edge until only about 12″–14″ of the quilt is exposed.

Generally, this is not necessary on small sections, but with a large quilt, it is almost always necessary to roll it up like a sleeping bag.

4. Move to the machine and position the end of the first seam you are quilting under the needle. Hold the remainder of the section in your lap.

If you have a needle-down position on your machine, engage it now. Let the first few stitches stitch in place. If your machine has an automatic process for locking stitches, take advantage of that at the beginning and end of each complete row.

As you begin to quilt, use both hands to pull away from the seam, creating the ditch in which you will stitch. Because you are working on a small piece, the addition of extra tables and work surface is probably not as necessary as it would be for a large quilt.

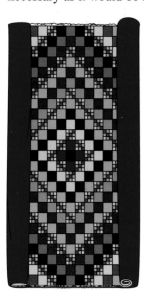 

You can eliminate the sleeping bag roll by quilting large quilts in small sections.

5. When you have finished the first seam, re-roll the section and prepare to quilt the center horizontal seam. After that, I usually continue to work outward from the center, sewing one or two horizontal seams on each side of the center, then switching back to sewing vertical seams, and so on. The bigger the section, the more likely you are to need to re-roll or re-package.

As you re-roll, trim thread ends, remove safety pins if you like, and check the quilt back for newly sewn tucks. It is not uncommon to find little puckers where seams cross. My decision is not to take the stitching out on those. I have found that you can often ease a little tuck out by pulling your fingernail across the pucker. (Small tucks are more likely to happen with polyester batting than with cotton. The polyester is slick, so the fabric can slide. With cotton batting, the quilt fabric and batting almost stick to each other.)

If your quilt section would be enhanced by adding free-motion quilting, just continue reading about free-motion quilting. If you were just practicing quilting and want to bind this piece, see binding details.

Free-Motion Quilting

Free-motion quilting means you can quilt in any direction without turning an entire quilt or section. It allows you almost complete control: you determine how fast the needle moves, how fast and where the fabric moves. It is usually done using the darning foot with the feed dogs down or covered.

Hand Position for Free-Motion Quilting

I see many people machine quilting with both hands on top of the fabric, basically pushing the fabric around. This is not bad for in-the-ditch quilting, where the machine pulls the fabric. It may even work for people when they do free-motion quilting, and it may work for you—but it doesn't work for me. If you have been buying every tool available to help move your layers, try this hand position instead.

My left hand is almost always under the layered quilt. Just grab the quilt from the back. It creates a slightly bunched area, but you don't hold in one place long enough to wrinkle. My right hand rolls up the edge and grabs it so that my hands are about six inches apart. Then I pull the fabric between my hands just enough to be taut. Most of the time, the fabric is actually raised off the surface of the machine so that the "drag" resulting from friction is reduced to a minimum. This is like having your quilt in a little hoop right where you are quilting. This position is especially easy with small quilts, blocks, and sections, but I use it with big quilts, too.

A Few Safety Tips

The end of the darning foot attachment used in free motion quilting does not actually touch the fabric, but is just above the surface. It will hold the fabric down when the force of the needle going up tries to pull the fabric along. The darning foot also warns you of exactly where the needle is going to go down. Sometimes, when you are moving the fabric around near the needle, it is easy to lose track of the exact position. Therefore, the foot does double duty. It tells you where you want the fabric to be and where you don't want your fingers to be.

If you have long hair, it is a good idea to pull it back. Again, in the rush of doing so many things at once, you can let your head get too close to the take-up lever and long hair can get caught.

Binding Your Quilt

Stabilizing the Quilt's Edges

Unless there is quilting very close to the edges of the quilt, it is a good idea to stabilize the quilt before adding the binding. Machine baste a scant ¼" from the raw edge of the quilt top. Stitch through the top, the batting and the backing on all four sides of the quilt. Excess batting and backing will be trimmed away later.

French-Fold Bindings

A French-fold binding feels great! It is double-folded, which gives extra body and strength to the binding. That means the fabric is cut four times as wide as the desired finished width of the binding plus ½" for two seam allowances, plus ⅛" to ¼" to go around the thickness of the quilt. The fatter the batt, the more you need to allow here. The length is determined by the size of the quilt.

My favorite finished width is whatever size I think looks best on a particular quilt. Some quilts need a subtle narrow binding and others look best with a wide, high contrast binding. The most common width for a bed quilt is about

½" finished. With that width and an average full-size quilt, a ½" binding requires about ¾ to ⅞ yard of fabric.

Should You Cut Bindings on the Crosswise or Lengthwise Grain, or on the Bias?

For years, I cut quilt binding on the lengthwise grain, unless it was for a curved edge; then it had to be cut on the bias. A few years ago, I was puzzling about the number of quilts I saw that had slightly rippled or flared final borders and now I have an alternate suggestion.

First, I encourage quilters to more carefully measure borders and to quilt borders as heavily as the interior of the quilt. If that has not controlled the last border, I encourage them to cut binding strips on the crosswise grain. Hold the binding taut—but not stretched—while sewing it in place. When the binding relaxes, there is slight shrinkage that helps control the flare. Cutting binding on the crosswise grain means you will need to piece more often to create enough overall length. Use a diagonal seam to avoid adding excess bulk. We recommend using the **From Marti Michell** Corner Trimmer #8064 to cut perfect angles on the ends of the strips.

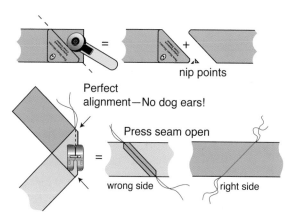

Blunt or Mitered Corners?

For years, I was very happy with blunt corners on most of my bindings and those were the only instructions I gave. However, if I were to enter quilts in competition, I knew I would take the time to make mitered corners—not because I like mitered corners better or because I love the recipient of the quilt enough to do a bit more work. Only because I know most judges give more points for mitered corner bindings.

In the last few years, peer pressure has caused me to reconsider and now my quilts have continuous bindings with mitered corners, so I am including those instructions

in this book. Interestingly, even though I machine piece and machine quilt nearly every quilt, I still love a hand-finished binding. That is, it is stitched onto the right side of the quilt by machine and wraps around the edge of the quilt to the back, where it is sewn by hand with a blind stitch.

Adding Continuous Binding with Mitered Corners

The length of the binding strip must be equal to the total distance around the quilt plus about 12″ to 15″. Fold the binding strip in half lengthwise with the wrong sides touching and the raw edges even.

1. Lay the binding on the quilt top so that both raw edges of binding match the raw edge of the quilt top. In the middle of one edge, make a diagonal fold in the binding and let the raw end hang off the quilt. Start stitching.

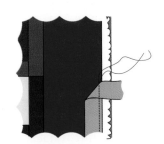

2. At the corner, stop stitching ¼″ from the edge of the quilt top. Secure stitching in your favorite way and remove the quilt from the machine.

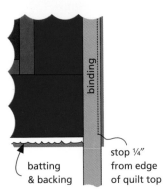

batting & backing

stop ¼″ from edge of quilt top

3. Fold binding away from the quilt, making a perfect 45-degree angle.

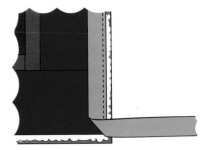

4. Fold binding back onto the next edge of the quilt. The new fold should be even with the binding edge just sewn. Start sewing again from the folded edge of the binding.

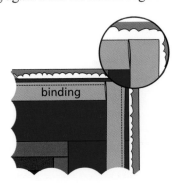

binding

5. Continue around the quilt, repeating this process at every corner. Overlap the binding at the starting point and fold so it hangs off, as in step 1. Trim away binding ends.

6. Trim away excess batting and backing.

7. Roll the binding around the raw edge of the quilt and hand stitch in place using the row of machine stitching as a guide. Fold the back side of the mitered corner into a miter and stitch it in place.

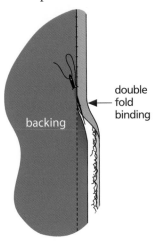

backing

double fold binding

Signing Your Quilt

A quilt is not done until it is signed. Make a label for the back of your quilt and record your name, the date and any other information you'd like. More and more machines have fancy stitches, easy-to-use alphabets and monogram or embroidery capabilities. Look to these as opportunities to add creative interest to labels.

What Size is a Bed Quilt?

Many quilts are made for the fun of making them and the size doesn't matter. Quilts of any size can be used creatively on beds, sofa backs, walls, rolled and tucked in baskets, stacked in chifforobe displays. Size only matters much if you want a quilt to fit a bed, especially a specific bed. Then, you will be happiest with the results if you plan to make the quilt the size you want.

Start by making the bed just as you will later. Place a large sheet on top of all the bedding. Let the sheet hang as far down on a dust ruffle as you like. Make a pillow tuck or smooth out the quilt and stack the pillows on top, as you prefer. Pin up the sheet's edges as necessary to achieve just the right side coverage and drape. When you are satisfied, remove and measure the sheet. Add a couple of inches in both directions for take-up during quilting. This size is your goal for the finished quilt. I say goal because you must be prepared to compromise.

If you start looking at quilt sizes in magazines and books, you will notice very few quilts relate to a bed's size. To fit a bed, you may have to make more blocks. Certain block sizes won't repeat exactly as you desire, so you may have to adjust sashes or border widths. If you want the border to be the same width on all four sides of the quilt, you may have to make the interior of the quilt longer than you had planned. Happily, simply changing border widths can usually create the size quilt you want.

My Personal Quilt Size Guidelines

When measuring the bed isn't an option, I use these quilt size guidelines. They were developed by adding 9″ for a pillow tuck at one narrow end and a 13″ drop to the other three sides of the most common standard mattress sizes in the United States.

Twin	65″ x 97″ (165.1 cm x 246.4 cm)
Double	80″ x 97″ (203.2 cm x 246.4 cm)
Queen	86″ x 102″ (218.4 cm x 259.1 cm)
Queen/Double	84″ x 100″ (213.4 cm x 254 cm)
King	104″ x 102″ (264.2 cm x 259.1 cm)

In recent years, a new taller luxury mattress has appeared and, depending on your desired look, it might require a longer drop than 13″ on three sides. Also, if you don't want a pillow tuck, don't allow for one.

If you have a different size mattress, make a diagram similar to those on this page. It will give you a feeling for the percentage of the design that shows on the surface of the bed.

Add 9″ (22.9 cm)
Add 13″ **Twin Bed Mattress 39″ x 75″ (99 cm x190.5 cm)** Add 13″
Add 13″ (33 cm)

65″ x 97″ (165.1 cm x 246.4 cm)

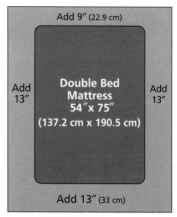

Add 9″ (22.9 cm)
Add 13″ **Double Bed Mattress 54″x 75″ (137.2 cm x 190.5 cm)** Add 13″
Add 13″ (33 cm)

80″ x 97″ (203.2 cm x 246.4 cm)

Add 9″ (22.9 cm)
Add 13″ **Queen Bed Mattress 60″x 80″ (152.4 cm x 203.2 cm)** Add 13″
Add 13″ (33 cm)

86″ x 102″ (218.4 cm x 259.1 cm)

Add 9″ (22.9 cm)
Add 13″ **King Bed Mattress 78″x 80″ (198.1 cm x 203.2 cm)** Add 13″
Add 13″ (33 cm)

104″ x 102″ (264.2 cm x 259.1 cm)

Resources

At press time, the following contact information was accurate. If there have been any changes since that time, we regret any inconvenience.

ASN Publishing
American School of Needlework, Inc.
DRG Publishing
306 E. Parr Road
Berne, IN 46711
www.anniesattic.com

Sew Steady
P. O. Box 10585
Eugene, OR 97402
(800) 837-3261
www.sewsteady.com
Sewing machine acrylic platform

Hobbs Bonded Fibers
200 South Commerce Drive
Waco, TX 76710
www.hobbsbondedfibers.com
Hobbs batting

Kwik Klip™
Paula Jean Creations
2827 Echo Way
Sacramento, CA 95821
(916) 488-3480
www.paulajeancreations.com

Maywood Studio
Distributed by E. E. Schenck
6000 N. Cutter Circle
Portland, OR 97217
www.maywoodstudio.com

Michell Marketing, Inc.
P. O. Box 80218
Chamblee, GA 30366
(770) 458-6500
www.frommarti.com
From Marti Michell *patterns, templates, books, rulers. Please ask for these products at your favorite quilt shop.*

Shades Textiles
119 W. Central Avenue
Griffin, GA 30223
www.shadestextiles.co
Shadestextiles@me.com
(770) 919-9824
Hand-dyed fabrics, kits, appliqué patterns, Shades SoftFuse

Entire contents © 2004 Martha G. Michell
All Rights Reserved

First Printing October 2004
Eleventh Printing January 2021
Printed in the U.S.A.